DORLING KINDERSLEY [DK] EYEWITNESS BOOKS

KNIGHT

Selection of medieval arrowheads

16th-century French gilt wall sconce

15th-century Flemish gold brooch

Late-medieval chamber pot

German fluted armor, c. 1520

Pricket candlestick c. 1230

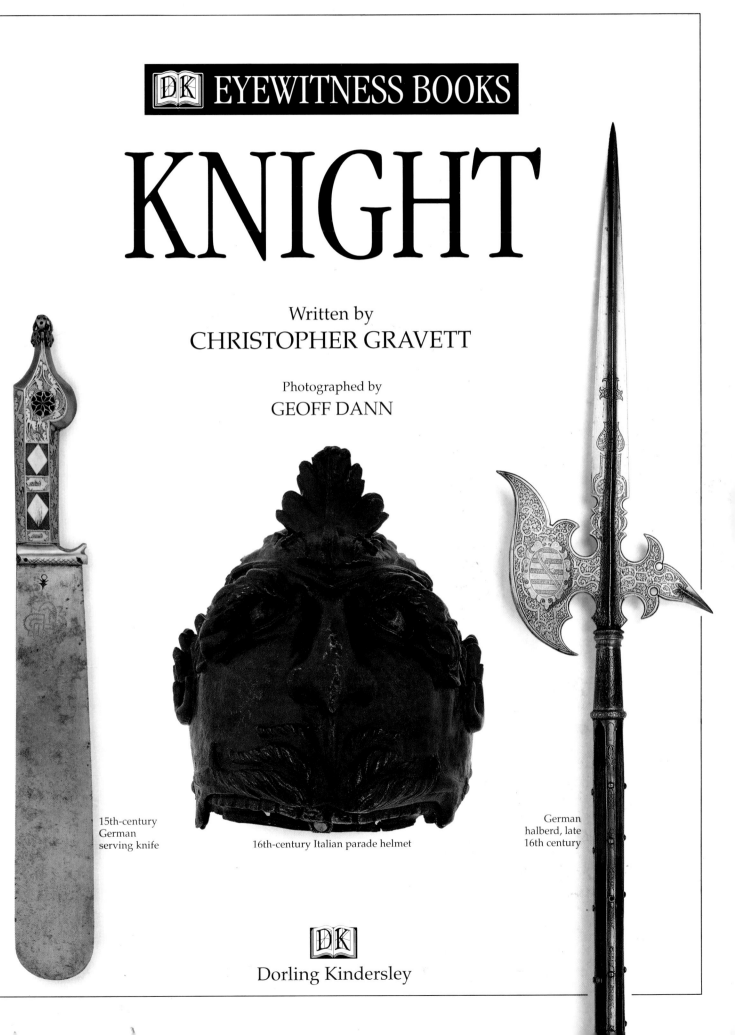

DK EYEWITNESS BOOKS

KNIGHT

Written by
CHRISTOPHER GRAVETT

Photographed by
GEOFF DANN

15th-century
German
serving knife

16th-century Italian parade helmet

German
halberd, late
16th century

Dorling Kindersley

15th-century
spur

15th-century German chanfron
(armor for horse's head)

Plaque from a tomb ornament
showing a knight on horseback

15th-century
Italian barbute

Dorling Kindersley

LONDON, NEW YORK, AUCKLAND, DELHI, JOHANNESBURG,
MUNICH, PARIS and SYDNEY

For a full catalog, visit

www.dk.com

Project editor Phil Wilkinson
Art editor Ann Cannings
Managing editor Helen Parker
Managing art editor Julia Harris
Production Louise Barratt
Picture research Kathy Lockley

This Eyewitness ® Book has been conceived by
Dorling Kindersley Limited and Editions Gallimard

© 1993 Dorling Kindersley Limited
This edition © 2000 Dorling Kindersley Limited
First American edition, 1993

Published in the United States by
Dorling Kindersley Publishing, Inc.
95 Madison Avenue
New York, NY 10016
2 4 6 8 10 9 7 5 3 1

Dorling Kindersley books are available at special discounts for bulk
purchases for sales promotions or premiums. Special editions, including
personalized covers, excerpts of existing guides, and corporate imprints
can be created in large quantities for specific needs. For more
information, contact Special Markets Dept., Dorling Kindersley
Publishing, Inc., 95 Madison Ave., New York, NY 10016;
Fax: (800) 600-9098

Library of Congress Cataloging-in-Publication Data
Gravett, Christopher.
Knight / written by Christopher Gravett.
p. cm. — (Eyewitness Books)
Includes index.
Summary: Discusses the age of knighthood, covering such aspects as
arms, armor, training, ceremonies, tournaments and the code of chivalry,
and the Crusades.
1. Knights and knighthood — Juvenile literature.
2. Arms and armor — Juvenile literature. 3. Civilization,
Medieval — Juvenile literature.
[1. Knights and knighthood. 2. Civilization, Medieval.] I.Title.
CR4513.D36 2000 940.1—dc20 92-1590
ISBN 0-7894-5875-6 (pb)
ISBN 0-7894-5874-8 (hc)

Color reproduction by Colourscan, Singapore
Printed in China by Toppan Printing Co. (Shenzhen) Ltd.

German
halberd,
c 1500

16th-
century
German
sword

Contents

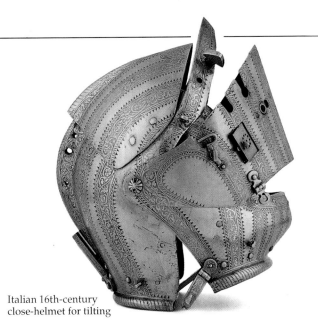

Italian 16th-century
close-helmet for tilting

The first knights

In the fourth century A.D. the Roman Empire fell and Europe was invaded by various barbarian tribes. One of the dominant groups was the Franks of central and western Europe, who gradually expanded their power until, in A.D. 800, their leader Charlemagne (right) became emperor of the West. Charlemagne and his forebears added to the number of horsemen in their army, giving land to mounted warriors. In the ninth century the empire, torn by civil wars and invasions, broke up. Powerful local lords and their mounted warriors offered protection to peasants, who became their serfs in return. In this feudal system, which first developed in western Europe, the lords themselves owed allegiance to greater lords, and all were bound by oaths of loyalty. All these lords, and some of the men who served them, were knights – warriors who fought on horseback. By the 11th century a new social order was formed by armored knights, who served a local lord, count, or duke, and were in turn served by serfs.

WINGED SPEAR *right*
Charlemagne's infantrymen (foot soldiers) usually carried spears with lugs that stuck out; but cavalrymen (mounted warriors) may have used smaller versions as well. The lugs could keep a weapon from sliding down the shaft, or prevent the spear from getting stuck in an opponent's body. They might also have helped if the spear was used for fencing.

CAROLINGIAN CAVALRY
Under Charlemagne and his descendants, the Carolingians, armored horsemen became more and more important. In this late-ninth-century manuscript the men have coats of scale armor, helmets, shields, and spears. They now ride with stirrups for a more secure seat. The man in front carries a dragon banner shaped like a wind sock.

Sharp, double-edged blade

Lug

Socket to insert shaft

BARBARIAN HORSEMAN
When the Roman Empire broke up, many horsemen from eastern Europe arrived in the west. This plaque shows a Lombard horseman of about 600. Unlike a later knight, he uses no stirrups or saddle, but horsemen like him were the forerunners of the mounted warriors of later centuries.

Double-edged blade

Iron crossguard

Tang of blade, missing its wooden grip

CUTTING EDGE

The double-edged slashing sword was the most highly prized of weapons and the most difficult and expensive to make. At first only wealthy people, such as those with enough money for a war-horse, could afford one, so the sword became the typical weapon of the knight.

Flaring blade

BATTLE-AX

The ax with a flaring blade developed in northern Europe. It was especially popular with the Vikings, who fought on foot, but lost favor with European mounted knights. Used by well-drilled infantry, it could prove lethal to horsemen, especially when mounted on a yard-long haft (handle) and swung in both hands.

KINGS AND NOBLES

The king and all his nobles were knights; there were also some knights who were not members of the nobility. In this 10th-century scene the king sits in close conference with his nobles, the men whose armed might kept him on the throne.

AX HEAD

Many of the tribes living in Europe after the fall of Rome fought on foot. The increase in mounted warfare was gradual. This ax head is from Germany, where feudalism and knighthood were slow in coming.

CHARGE!

Cavalrymen sent their opponents flying in this Italian manuscript of 1028. All the knights wear coats of mail (pp. 12–13) with mail hoods and iron helmets. Straps around the horses' chests and hindquarters hold their saddles in place. These warriors look like tough, practical fighting men rather than the courteous knights of chivalry.

The Normans

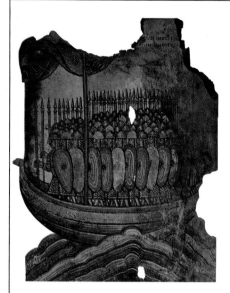

IN AN ATTEMPT to stop Viking raids on his territory in northern France, King Charles the Simple gave some land to a group of these northern invaders in 911. Their new home was called Normandy ("the land of the Northmen"), and their leader, Rollo, became its first duke. The Vikings fought on foot, but the Normans, as they became known, copied the French use of mounted knights and became formidable fighters. When King Edward the Confessor of England died in 1066, his cousin, Duke William of Normandy, claimed he had been promised the English throne. So he invaded with an army. He defeated the new king, Harold, in battle near Hastings and brought knights, castles, and the feudal system to England. At about the same time, Norman adventurers invaded parts of southern Italy and Sicily.

Metal boss

SHIELDED FROM DANGER
This little 12th-century bronze figurine shows that knightly equipment changed only slowly after the Norman Conquest. The top of the helmet is tilted slightly forward, and the figure wears a long undergarment below the mailcoat, on which long sleeves are now common. The shield has a decorative metal boss in the center.

Prick

Leather straps were originally attached here

PRICK SPUR
This 11th-century prick spur, made of tin-plated iron, was fastened to the knight's foot by straps riveted to its arms. Although spurs came to be worn by many different classes, they were always especially associated with knights.

Arm

Position of band to attach strap

Mouthpiece

Double-edged cutting blade

RIDING TO THE ATTACK *above*
This is a scene from the Bayeux Tapestry, an embroidery probably made within 10 years of the Battle of Hastings. It shows Norman knights, who wear mailcoats with hoods and iron helmets with noseguards. They carry kite-shaped shields, swords, and light lances. The small flags, called pennons, on the lances show them to be men of high rank.

SHIELD WALL
In this scene from the Bayeux Tapestry, the English defend their hilltop position at Hastings. Unlike the Normans, the English fought wholly on foot. The armor and weapons of the higher-ranking troops are similar to those of the Normans, except for the large two-handed ax at the shoulder of the left-hand figure. Bundles of javelins and a flying mace can be seen. Norman arrows have stuck in their shields.

SOLID FAITH
The Normans used stone not only to build some of their castles (pp. 22–23), but also for large cathedrals, abbeys, and churches throughout their newly conquered English kingdom. They used the Romanesque style of architecture, which was fashionable in Europe in the 11th and 12th centuries. Typical of the style were massive columns and rounded arches, seen here in the nave of Durham Cathedral.

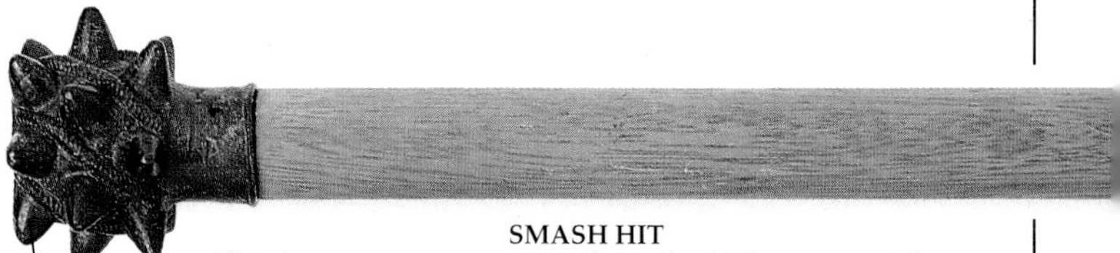

SMASH HIT
This bronze mace may date from the 12th century; it has been given a modern haft. The molded knobs could break an opponent's bones under flexible chain mail.

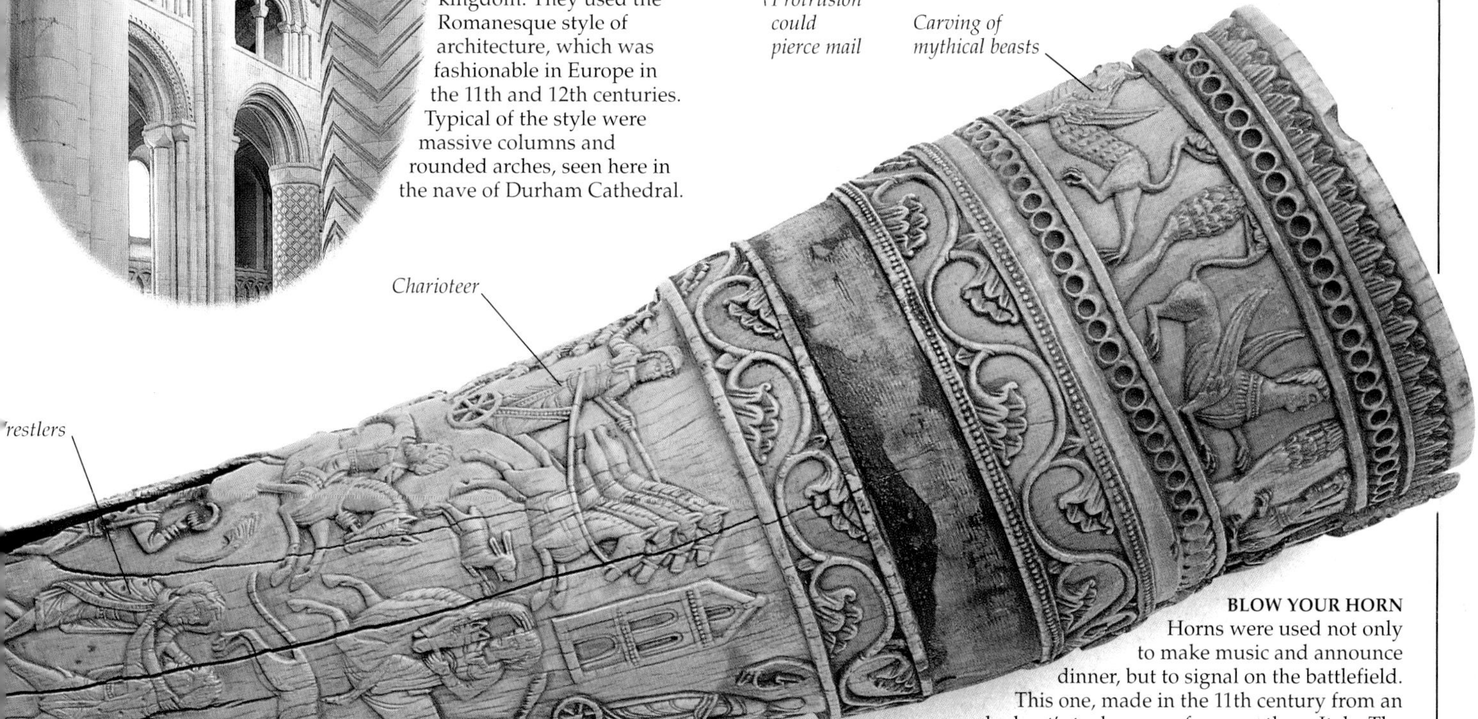

Protrusion could pierce mail

Carving of mythical beasts

Charioteer

restlers

BLOW YOUR HORN
Horns were used not only to make music and announce dinner, but to signal on the battlefield. This one, made in the 11th century from an elephant's tusk, comes from southern Italy. The Normans settled much of this area and conquered Sicily. Because it lay on profitable trade routes across the Mediterranean the island had a rich mixture of Byzantine and Muslim culture.

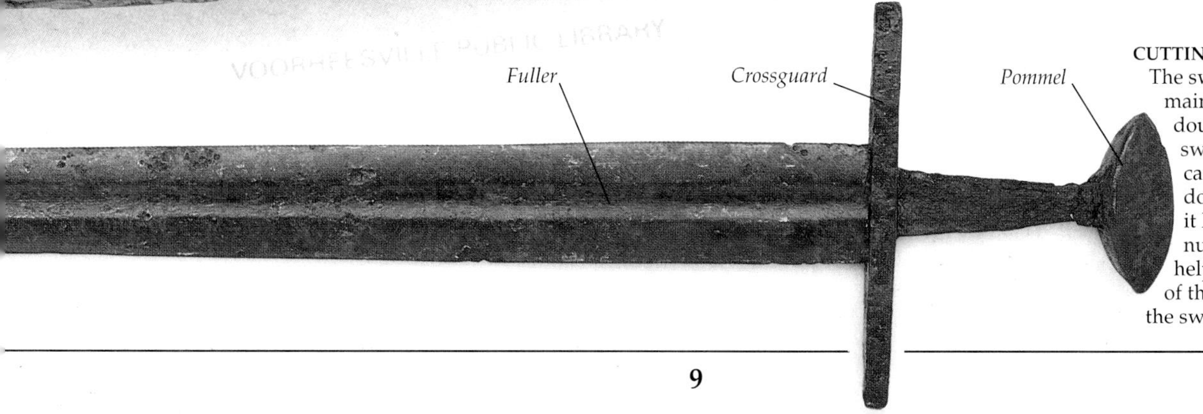

CUTTING EDGE
The sword was the knight's main weapon. This double-edged cutting sword has a groove, called a fuller, running down the blade to make it lighter. The brazil-nut-shaped pommel helps counter the weight of the blade and so makes the sword easier to handle.

Fuller *Crossguard* *Pommel*

Making a knight

WHEN HE WAS ABOUT SEVEN a boy of noble birth who was going to become a knight was usually sent away to a nobleman's household, often that of his uncle or a great lord, to be a page. Here he learned how to behave and how to ride. At about 14 he was apprenticed to a knight whom he served as a squire. He was taught how to handle weapons and how to look after his master's armor and horses; he even went into battle with the knight, helping him to put on his armor and assisting him if he was hurt or unhorsed. He learned how to shoot a bow and to carve meat for food. Successful squires were knighted when they were around 21 years old.

Backplate

Breastplate

THE PAGE
Sons of noble families who were sent away at a very early age to the household of a great lord or to the king's court learned a variety of skills. They were trained to serve a knight, to attend noble ladies, and to learn the art of courtly manners and good behaviour.

BOY'S CUIRASS
These pieces of armor of about 1600 are part of a full armor custom-made to fit a boy. Only rich families could afford to give their young sons such a gift.

Holes to attach tassets (thigh pieces)

PRACTICE MAKES PERFECT
Young men who wanted to be knights had to keep fit. So squires trained constantly to exercise their muscles and improve their skill with weapons. They practiced with each other and also sometimes with their knightly masters, who also needed to keep in shape. Such training was hard and not everyone could manage it. Those who did eventually went on to become knights. This 15th-century picture shows various ways the young men could train.

Putting (throwing) the stone

Throwing the javelin

Acrobatics

Fighting with sword and buckler

Fighting with quarterstaff

Wrestling

CHAUCER'S SQUIRE *above*
Geoffrey Chaucer wrote his *Canterbury Tales* in the late 1300s. One of the stories is told by a squire, who is the lively son of a knight and about 20 years old. He can compose songs, dance, draw, and write. He is also a good rider and knows how to joust. Other stories show that some squires were not as well-mannered as Chaucer's. Sometimes they behaved like thugs. At Boston, England, in 1288, two gangs of squires, pretending to hold a squires' tournament, burnt down half the town.

THE SQUIRE

The word "squire" comes from the French word *écuyer*, which meant "shield-bearer." In the 11th and 12th centuries many squires seem to have been servants of a lower social class, but later the sons of noble families became squires before being knighted. In the 13th century becoming a knight was so expensive that many young men tried to avoid actually being knighted and remained squires. Later "squire" came to mean a gentleman who owned land.

AT THE PEL
Squires could practice against a pel, or wooden post. Sometimes they were given weapons double the weight of those used in battle; this got them used to weapons, and developed their muscles.

AT THE TABLE
Chaucer notes how the squire carved the meat in front of his father at the dining table. Knowing how to carve properly was a skill taught to these sons of noble families as a part of their training.

Thigh-length leather boots

DUBBING
A squire was finally made into a knight at the ceremony of dubbing. This was originally a blow to the neck with the hand; by the 13th century the blow was replaced by a tap with the sword. The knight's sword and spurs were fastened on, and celebrations might follow when he could show off his skills. Another knight, often the squire's master or even the king, performed the dubbing.

JOUSTING PRACTICE *above*
This could be done with a wooden structure called a quintain, sometimes shaped like a soldier. After striking the shield at the end of the swinging arm the rider had to pass by quickly to avoid the swinging weight.

Iron, iron, everywhere

THE MAIN BODY ARMOR worn by early knights was made of mail, consisting of many small, linked iron rings. During the 12th century, knights started to wear more mail; their sleeves got longer, and mail leggings became popular. A padded garment called an aketon was also worn below the mail to absorb blows. In the 14th century knights added steel plates to protect their limbs, and the body was often protected further with a coat-of-plates, made of pieces of iron riveted to a cloth covering. By about 1400 some knights wore full suits of plate armor. A suit weighed about 44-55 lb (20-25 kg), and the weight was spread over the body so that a fit man could run, lie down, or mount a horse unaided in his armor. Stories of cranes being used to winch knights into the saddle are pure fantasy. But armor did have one major drawback: The wearer quickly became very hot.

MAIL
In this piece of mail, each open ring is interlinked with four others and closed with a rivet. A mail coat weighed about 20-31 lb (9-14 kg), and most of the weight was taken on the knight's shoulders. As mail was flexible, a heavy blow could cause broken bones or bruising.

KNIGHTLY PLAQUE
This mounted knight of the 14th century has a helm fitted with a crest. This helped to identify him in battle. However, by this time headgear like this was losing popularity in favor of the basinet and visor.

MAIL MAKER
No one knows exactly how mail was made. This 15th-century picture shows an armorer using pliers to join the links. Garments were shaped by increasing or reducing the number of links in each row, rather like stiches in modern knitting.

Pin allowing visor to be removed

Cord allowing mail to be removed

BASINET
This Italian basinet of the late 14th century was originally fitted with a visor that pivoted over the brow. But, probably within the helmet's working life, a side-pivoting visor was fitted. The Germans called this type of helmet a *Hundsgugel* (hound's hood).

Ventilation holes

Modern mail neck guard

COURTLY GAUNTLETS
Gauntlet plates, like this late-14th-century pair from Milan, Italy, were riveted to the back of a leather glove. Smaller plates were added to protect the fingers. On these plates each cuff has a band of brass on which is written the latin word AMOR, love.

Light horsemen, who might not
wear armor on their lower
legs, often wore helmets
like this German sallet
of 1480-1510. It was
originally fitted
with a chin
strap.

*Visor with
horizontal sight*

THE COMING OF PLATE ARMOR
The knight on the left dates from
about 1340. Over his padded aketon
he wears a mail coat and over that a
coat-of-plates. His surcoat is short
and his legs have some plate armor.
The knight on the right dates from
about 1420 and has full plate armor.

BARBUTE
Italian barbutes, like this one of about 1445, look
rather like ancient Greek Corinthian helmets.
The rosette-headed rivets secured a canvas lining
and inside, to which was sewn a padded lining.
Rivets lower down originally held a leather chin
strap to keep the helmet from being knocked off.

*"Gothic-style"
fluted decoration*

Pointed cuff

Center plate

Articulated plates

*Shaped knuckle
plate*

UNHORSED
Fully mailed knights needed to protect themselves against
heavy blows from lances or maces. This picture, drawn by
Matthew Paris in the first half of the 13th century, shows the
large shields they used. By 1400, thanks to the effectiveness
of plate armor, shields had become much smaller.

THE MAILED KNIGHT
This knight of about 1250 wears a
cloth surcoat over his mail, perhaps in imitation
of Muslim dress seen on crusade (pp. 54–55).
His mail sleeves are extended into mittens, with
leather palms to give a good grip.

GAUNTLET
This shows the long, fluted style
popular for German "Gothic" armor of
the later 15th century. The missing
finger and thumb plates would be
riveted to a glove attached inside. Plate
armor like this gave better protection
than mail, because it was solid and did
not flex when struck by a weapon.

Fashion in steel

By the 15th century, knights were protecting themselves with full suits of plate armor. The armor's smooth surface deflected the edges and points of weapons. This reduced the impact of any blows but still allowed the armor to be made reasonably light. Plate armor was often made to imitate civilian fashions. Some armours were partly painted black, both to preserve the metal and as a decoration. Or armor could be "blued" by controlled heating of the metal. Some pieces were engraved with a pointed tool, and from the 16th century on, designs were often etched into the metal with acid. Gold plating, or gilding, was sometimes used to embellish borders or bands of decoration and, in some cases, entire armors.

"Bellows" visor, so-called because of its shape

Shoulder defense made from several articulated (individually moving) plates

Besague to guard the armpit

"Wing" on the poleyn, or knee guard, protected the wearer from side cuts

PUCKER SUIT
The ridges in this German armor of about 1520 imitate the pleated clothing of the time. The style is called "Maximilian" after the German emperor, although he does not seem to have been connected with it. It combines the rounded Italian style with the fluted German decoration of the 15th century. This form of armor remained popular until about 1530. This suit is made up of surviving pieces from several similar armors of the same period.

Blued, etched, and gilt wings

Embossed, etched and gilt dolphin's mask placed over fish-tailed scrolls

OPEN TO THE AIR
The burgonet was an open-faced helmet that allowed more air to reach the face than the close-helmet below. This example, with its decoration imitating the art of ancient Rome, was intended for use in parades rather than for warfare. It was made in Augsburg, Germany, in about 1520.

Burgonet

Cherubs' head

Visor pivots at the same point as the rest of the face guard

Peg for lifting visor

PROTECTING THE FACE
A close-helmet is one with a visor to protect the wearer's face. This one was probably made in France in about 1575. It is covered with embossed decoration, which was usually added to armor made for parades.

Figures in Roman armor

Sleeping lion

Close-helmet

Gorget plates attached to the buffe protect the throat

Slim plates on this falling buffe may be lowered over one another to allow more air to reach the face

rge pauldrons made of veral strips of steel joined ernally by leather straps, ich let them move

nce rest helped pport the weight of e lance and keep it m being rammed ough the armpit impact

Reinforcing breast (plackart) attached to the breastplate to increase protection against firearms

Small plates on the gauntlets give complete freedom of movement to the hand

Poleyn has plates above and below, which allow the knee to bend without exposing the cloth beneath

TEST FASHION
is armor was made for Lord ckhurst in about 1587. It is product of the workshops Greenwich set up by nry VIII. The breastplate s followed the fashion in coming more and more inted at the waist until, here, the full shape own as a peascod is rmed. The bulging hips ow for thick underwear rn beneath. The burgonet s a triple-barred face- ard behind a removable ffe.

Flexible sabaton leaves the sole exposed so the shoe beneath does not skid

TRIUMPHAL ENTRY
This picture of King Louis XII of France entering Quenes was painted about 1510. The colored cloth skirts popular at the time were called bases. The king's helmet is fitted with a heraldic crest.

MASTER DRAWING
Jacob Halder, who was master armourer at Greenwich, near London, produced illustrations for people who wanted armor made. They were often in the form of a set of pieces called a garniture which could be made into armors for war and tournament. This one was for Sir Henry Lee, master of the armouries from 1578 to 1610.

ON PARADE
Three knights ride in procession, from the early 16th-century *Triumph of Maximilian*. They carry enormous parade banners representing Styria, Austria, and Old Austria. The horses wear plate armor; the animal in the middle even has pieces to guard his upper legs – such items were very rare.

Armor, the inside story

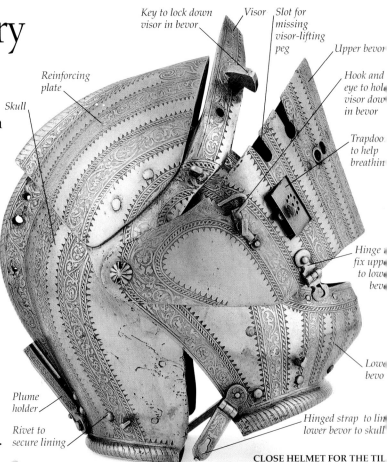

PEOPLE OFTEN THINK that plate armor is clumsy and stiff. But if it were, it would be little use on the battlefield. In fact, a man in armor could do just about anything a man can do when not wearing it. The secret lies in the way armorers made the plates so that they could move with each other and with the wearer. Some plates were attached to each other with a rivet, which allowed the two parts to pivot (turn) at that point. Others were joined by a sliding rivet, one part of which was set not in a round hole but in a slot, so the two plates could move in and out. Internal leather connecting straps, called leathers, also allowed this type of movement. Tube-shaped plates could also have "flanged" edge, or projecting rim, to fit inside the edge of another tubular plate so that they could twist around.

Key to lock down visor in bevor
Visor
Slot for missing visor-lifting peg
Reinforcing plate
Upper bevor
Skull
Hook and eye to hol visor dow in bevor
Trapdoo to help breathin
Hinge fix upp to low bevo
Plume holder
Rivet to secure lining
Low bevo
Hinged strap to lim lower bevor to skull

CLOSE HELMET FOR THE TIL
This etched North Italian helmet of about 1570 has a reinforcing pla riveted to the skull or bowl. The visor fits inside the bevor, which is divide into upper and lower parts. The visor and the two parts of the bevor a pivot at the same point on each side of the skull and can be locked togethe

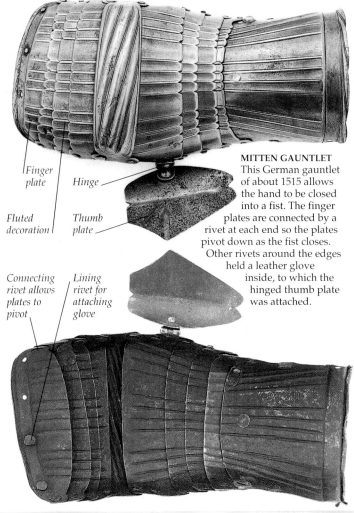

Finger plate
Hinge
Fluted decoration
Thumb plate

MITTEN GAUNTLET
This German gauntlet of about 1515 allows the hand to be closed into a fist. The finger plates are connected by a rivet at each end so the plates pivot down as the fist closes. Other rivets around the edges held a leather glove inside, to which the hinged thumb plate was attached.

Connecting rivet allows plates to pivot
Lining rivet for attaching glove

HOT WORK
This armorer has heated a piece o metal in a furnace to soften it and is hammering it into shape over a anvil set in a tree trunk. A bellow forces air over the fire to raise the temperature.

Connecting leather (replacement)
Couter

Hole for sprung stud on rear plate to close lower cannon

Hinge
Lower cannon of vambrace

16

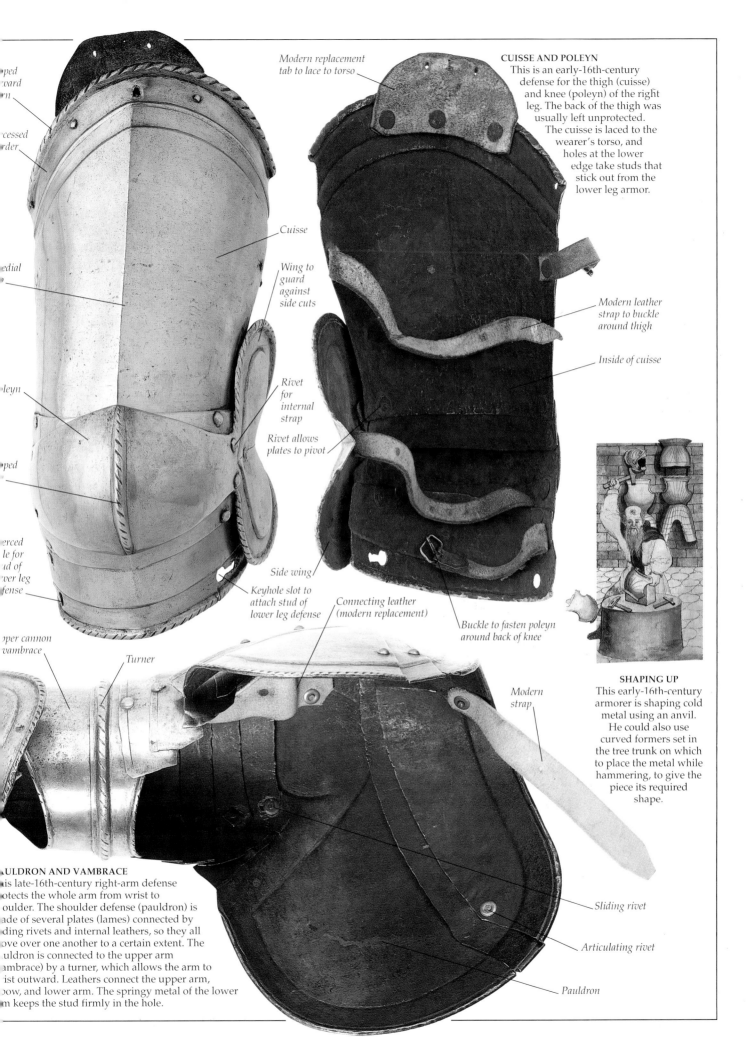

...ped
...vard
...n

...cessed
...rder

...edial

...leyn

...ped

...erced
...le for
...d of
...ver leg
...fense

Cuisse

Wing to guard against side cuts

Rivet for internal strap

Rivet allows plates to pivot

Side wing

Keyhole slot to attach stud of lower leg defense

Modern replacement tab to lace to torso

CUISSE AND POLEYN
This is an early-16th-century defense for the thigh (cuisse) and knee (poleyn) of the right leg. The back of the thigh was usually left unprotected. The cuisse is laced to the wearer's torso, and holes at the lower edge take studs that stick out from the lower leg armor.

Modern leather strap to buckle around thigh

Inside of cuisse

Connecting leather (modern replacement)

Buckle to fasten poleyn around back of knee

SHAPING UP
This early-16th-century armorer is shaping cold metal using an anvil. He could also use curved formers set in the tree trunk on which to place the metal while hammering, to give the piece its required shape.

...pper cannon
...vambrace

Turner

Modern strap

Sliding rivet

Articulating rivet

Pauldron

...ULDRON AND VAMBRACE
...is late-16th-century right-arm defense
...otects the whole arm from wrist to
...oulder. The shoulder defense (pauldron) is
...ade of several plates (lames) connected by
...ding rivets and internal leathers, so they all
...ove over one another to a certain extent. The
...uldron is connected to the upper arm
...ambrace) by a turner, which allows the arm to
...ist outward. Leathers connect the upper arm,
...bow, and lower arm. The springy metal of the lower
...m keeps the stud firmly in the hole.

Arms and the man

THE SWORD WAS THE most important knightly weapon, a symbol of knighthood itself. Until the late 13th century the double-edged cutting sword was used in battle. But as plate armor became more common more pointed swords became popular, because they were better for thrusting through the gaps between the plates. The mace, which could concuss an opponent, also became more popular. Before drawing his sword or using his mace, however, a mounted knight usually charged at his opponent with his lance lowered. Lances increased in length during the medieval period and, from about 1300, began to be fitted with circular vamplates to guard the hand. Other weapons such as the short ax could be used on horseback, while long-handled staff weapons, held in both hands, could be used on foot.

AT THE READY
The double-edged cutting sword, shown unsheathed in this 13th-century tomb effigy, could tear mail links apart and drive them into a wound.

THE COUCHED LANCE
Early 14th-century knights charge in formation with lances "couched" under their arms. To keep their line, they rode at a trot before charging as they neared the enemy.

SHINING SWORD
This sword of about 1460 has a copper-gilt crossguard. Like the weapon above it, it was probably made for a rich knight.

Copper-gilt crossguard

Fish-tail pommel   *Horn grip*

CUTTING A PATH *right*
This early-14th-century manuscript shows that double-edged swords were still widely used to slash at an enemy. Surviving skeletons show that the force of a blow could cause terrible injuries, even cutting bones.

Flange

FLANGED MACE
A flanged mace has ridges sticking out from the head to concentrate the force of the blow. Maces like this may have been used as early as the 11th century but became more popular in the 14th century as more plate armor was worn. This example has a bronze head mounted on a modern haft. An iron ball attached to a haft by a chain was called a flail; this was usually used on foot.

Mode haft

Make mark

Fish-tail pommel   *Modern cord grip*

GREAT SWORD
Two-hand swords were large versions of the ordinary sword and were swung in both hands to deliver a powerful blow. This one, possibly made in England, is from about 1450. Large swords began to become popular in the 13th century; a knight would often hang one from his saddle in addition to his normal sword.

Diamond-section blade

Diamond-profile blade

Cross-guard

Modern cord grip

Wheel pommel with cap

GETTING THE POINT
On this sharply pointed war sword of the second half of the 14th century, the old-style blade with a central groove or fuller has been replaced by a stiffer one with a diamond-shaped profile. This assisted the thrust. The acute point could burst apart the links of a piece of mail.

DEATH OR GLORY
Two riders slammed together at about 60 mph (96 km/h); this made the pointed lance lethal. In this early-15th-century picture a knight's lance has passed by his opponent's shield and punched through his armor. The figure on the left has a heavy-bladed cutting sword called a falchion. A pole-ax, a staff weapon used on foot, lies on the ground.

WEAPON OF RANK
This sword was probably made for a wealthy person. Dating from the late 15th century, it has a sunken hollow in the pommel that would have held a plaque with the owner's coat of arms.

Fig-shaped pommel

Hollow for small shield

BLOODY BUSINESS
When a dagger was used the opponent was often grasped around the neck before the fatal blow was struck. This often meant stabbing at the face or, as in this late-15th-century picture, cutting the throat. Like sharply pointed swords, such daggers could also pierce mail.

SHORT AX
Knights sometimes wielded two-handed axes, but the smaller, single-handed variety was easier to use on horseback. This 14th-century example, mounted on a modern haft, has the remains of long iron langets which ran down the haft to stop the ax head being cut off. The back is extended to form a beak.

Part of langet

Single-edged blade

Remains of gilt decoration

Rondel

DAGGER
Knights did not use daggers very much until the 14th century. This is a late-15th-century rondel dagger, so-called because of the protective iron discs at either end of the grip. It was the typical knightly dagger and was carried in a decorated leather sheath.

On horseback

THE HORSE was an expensive but vital part of a knight's equipment. Knights needed horses for warfare, hunting, jousting, traveling, and carrying baggage. The most costly animal was the destrier, or war-horse. This was a stallion about the size of a modern heavy hunter. Its deep chest gave it staying power yet it was also nimble. Knights prized war-horses from Italy, France, and Spain. In fact the Spanish Andalusian is more like a war-horse than any other modern kind is. By the 13th century, knights usually had at least two war-horses, plus other horses for different tasks. The courser was a swift hunting horse, though this name was sometimes applied to the war-horse, with "destrier" used for the jousting horse. For travel, knights often used a well-bred, easy-paced mount called a palfrey. Sumpter horses carried baggage.

FIT FOR A KING
An early-14th-century miniature shows the king of England on his war-horse. The richly decorated covering, or trapper, could be used to display heraldic arms and might be padded for extra protection. Some were even made of mail. Notice the "fan" crest.

GREAT HORSE
A destrier, or "great horse," wears armor on its head, neck, and chest, the latter partly covered in decorative cloth. The knight in this 15th-century picture wears long spurs and shows the straight-legged riding position. He uses double reins, one of which is highly decorated.

Etched and gilt decoration

"Eye" for leathers

Separately moving metal plates

Tread

MINIATURE GOAD
A knight wore spurs on his feet, and used them to urge on his horse. This 12th- or 13th-century prick spur is made of tin-plated iron. The two leather straps that passed over and under the foot were riveted to the ends of each spur arm.

Prick or goad

Rowel

ROWEL SPUR *right*
Spurs with a rotating spiked rowel on the end of the arm had replaced prick spurs by the early 14th century. This decorated copper-gilt example is from the second half of the 15th century.

FIRM SEAT
Iron stirrups like this one dating from the 14th century were worn with long straps so the knight was almost standing in them. This, together with the support of high saddle boards at front and rear, meant he had a very secure seat from which to fight.

Spike with spiral pattern

Brass plume-holder

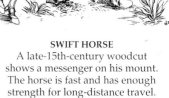

SWIFT HORSE
A late-15th-century woodcut shows a messenger on his mount. The horse is fast and has enough strength for long-distance travel.

Flanged eyeguard

NOBLE HEAD
Horse armor was expensive and uncommon. If a knight could only afford part of the armor, he would usually choose the shaffron, the piece for the head. The shaffron probably came into use during the 12th century. This one, complete with crinet to protect the neck, is northern Italian and dates from about 1570. Both pieces are decorated with etched and gilt bands depicting animals and mythical figures. The crinet flexes on sliding rivets and internal leathers.

Noseguard

15TH-CENTURY JOUSTER
"Destrier" – from atin *dextra*, "right hand" – may suggest the horse was led with the ight hand, or that he led with the right leg so that if he swerved he would move away rom an opponent.

Chain goes under horse's throat

Poll plate

Decorated metal boss

FROM THE HORSE'S MOUTH
Curb bits similar to this one were used by military riders from the later Middle Ages to the 19th century. Leverage from the long arms put pressure on the horse's mouth and gave good control.

UZZLE
steel frame is decorated with openwork panels and iseled bars. At the top, a German inscription reads s God wills, so is my aim." Below is a crowned imperial gle and the date 1561. Two lizards support the panel. The ters at the bottom probably indicate the owner's name.

Ring for rein

SHAFFRON *right*
This German shaffron from the 1460s has a poll plate, attached by a brass hinge, to protect the top of the horse's head. The central spike and rondel are missing. The rivets originally held an internal lining.

The castle

A CASTLE COULD BE a lord's private home and his business headquarters, as well as a base for his soldiers. The first castles probably appeared in northwestern France in the ninth century, because of civil wars and Viking attacks. Although some early castles were built of stone, many consisted of earthworks and timber walls. But slowly knights began to build castles of stone and later brick, because these materials were stronger and more fire-resistant. In the late 15th century, more settled societies, demand for comfort, and the increasing use of powerful cannons meant that castles became less important. Some of their military roles were taken over by forts, defended gun platforms controlled by the state.

NARROW SLIT
Windows near the ground were made very small to guard against enemy missiles or soldiers climbing through. Such windows were narrow on the outside but splayed on the inside to let in as much light as possible.

MOTTE AND BAILEY
The castles of the 10th to 12th centuries usually consisted of a ditch and rampart with wooden fences. From the 11th century on, many were also given a mound called a motte, a last line of defense with a wooden tower on top. The bailey, or courtyard, below it held all the domestic buildings.

STRENGTH IN STONE
Stone donjons, or keeps, became common in the late 11th and 12th centuries. The larger ones could hold accommodation for the lord and his household. The bailey was by now often surrounded by stone walls with square towers. Round towers appeared in the 12th century.

RINGS OF DEFENSE
Concentric castles, which were first built in the 13th century, had two rings of walls, one within the other. This gave two lines of defence. The inner ring was often higher to give archers a clear field of fire. Some old castles with keeps had outer rings, added later; these gave yet another line of defense. Sometimes rivers were used to give broad water defenses.

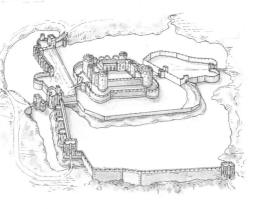

MEN AT WORK
Stone castles cost a fortune to build and could take years to complete. The lord and the master mason chose a strong site and plan. Stone had to be brought in specially. In addition, large amounts of lime, sand, and water were needed for the mortar. The materials and work force were normally provided by the lord.

CRACKING CASTLE
Sometimes wooden fences on the motte were replaced by stone walls, forming a shell keep. Occasionally a stone tower was built on a motte, but the artificial mound was not always strong enough to take the weight. The 13th-century Clifford's Tower in York, England, has cracked as a result.

GATEHOUSE
Castle gatehouses were always strongly fortified. At Dover, England, the gate is flanked by two massive round towers. The walls are splayed at the base; the thicker masonry helps to protect them against mining. There is also a deep dry ditch to obstruct attackers.

INSIDE A KEEP
A large keep like the one at Rochester had enough space to house the lord and his followers. The basement was used for storage. The first floor usually housed the garrison. The hall on the next floor was used by everyone to eat and in some cases sleep in. The lord's family had rooms on the top floor of the keep.

Wooden hoarding to allow soldiers to overlook the base of the wall

Spiral stone stairs

Chapel

Lord's apartments

Great hall

Guardrooms

Storerooms

GOOD SITE
This view of the keep at Rochester shows how it is surrounded by strong outer defensive walls.

GREAT TOWER
The keep, or donjon (from which comes the English word "dungeon", an underground prison), always had strong walls. At Rochester, begun in 1087, they are 12 ft (3.7 m) thick at the base and the tower is 70 ft (21 m) high. The entrance was always on the first floor and was often protected by a forebuilding. There was a well in the basement, to provide water if the garrison was trapped in the tower during a siege.

Merlon or battlement

Corner turret

Buttress to strengthen wall

Large upper window later made even larger

Merlon of forebuilding

Chapel window

Forebuilding with entrance doorway

Narrow slit on lower level, to protect against enemy missiles

Draw-bridge pit

23

The castle at war

CASTLES WERE BUILT as defense against enemy attacks. The first obstacle for the enemy was a ditch all the way around the castle, which was sometimes filled with stakes to slow a man down and make him an easy target. Moats – ditches that were often filled with water – were less common: they kept attackers from mining (burrowing) under the walls. Towers jutted out from the walls so that defending archers could shoot along the walls to repel any attackers. Small gates allowed the defenders to rush out and surprise the enemy. The castle was also used as a base from which knights rode out to fight an enemy or ravage his lands.

Iron-clad wooden portcullis

Wooden doors barred from behind

GATEHOUSE
The gatehouse was always strongly defended, as it was thought to be a weak spot. Usually a wooden lifting bridge spanned the ditch and an iron gate called a portcullis could be lowered to form a barrier

VAULTED CEILING
There are holes built into the stone vaulted ceiling of the castle gatehouse. These allowed people on the floor above to pour water down to put out fires, or possibly to drop stones or boiling water onto the heads of attackers.

Gap (or crenel), through which defenders could shoot

Merlon to protect defenders against missiles

Round flanking tower; the shape leaves no corners for a battering ram or miners

High turrets gave clear views of approaching enemies

Machicolations along gate tower

Battlement on section of curtain wall

OVER THE WALLS

This early 14th-century picture shows the 11th-century Crusader Godfrey of Bouillon attacking fortifications. His men are using scaling ladders, which was always dangerous because the defenders would try to push them away. Archers provide covering fire.

FLANKING TOWERS

This picture was taken looking up the front of the castle. Flanking towers jut out on either side to protect the gate. The battlements are thrust forward (machicolated) so that they overhang the walls. Boiling water or hot sand could be poured through the holes to hurt the attackers below. The holes could also be used to pour cold water, to put out fires.

Stone corbel supports the battlement

EMBRASURE

An embrasure was an alcove in the thickness of the wall, with a narrow opening, or "loophole," to the outside. This allowed defenders to look and shoot out without showing themselves. In this example, the rounded lower part of the loophole is designed for guns, used more and more in warfare by the time this castle was built.

AT SIEGE

Both the attackers and the defenders of this castle are using siege engines (pp. 26–27) to hurl missiles at each other.

KNIGHTLY STRONGHOLD

Bodiam Castle in Sussex, England, was built in 1385 by Sir Edward Dalyngrigge amid fears of a French invasion. It has a single stone curtain wall with round towers at the corners and is surrounded by a broad moat to protect the occupants. To guard against possible treachery among the defending soldiers, there are no connecting doors between their quarters and those of the lord.

Turret or watchtower

Lancet window to let in light but keep out missiles

Siege warfare

Counterpoise arm

Sling

Weighted box

An enemy attacking a castle would make a formal demand for the people inside to surrender. If this was rejected, he would try to take the castle by siege. There were two methods. The first was to surround the castle, keep people from leaving or going in, and starve the defenders into submission. The second was to use force. Attackers could tunnel under the wall and come up inside, or undermine the wall and bring it down. Alternatively, the attackers could try to break the walls down with battering rams, catapults, or, from the 14th century on, cannon. They could also try to get over the wall using scaling ladders or a moving tower fitted with a drawbridge that could be let down on the top of the wall.

Sling pouch

Rope to pull arm down again

TREBUCHET
The trebuchet was first used in Europe in the 12th century. It worked on the principle of counterpoise: There was a pivoting wooden arm with a heavy weight at one end and a sling, containing a missile such as a stone, at the other. As the weight dropped, the sling flew up, launching the missile toward the castle. Some trebuchets had arms about 60 ft (18 m) long. On average they could probably hurl stones of about 100-200 lb (45-90 kg) up to 980 ft (300 m).

Hauling rope

ASSAULT
Besiegers attack a fortress with scaling ladders while crossbowmen and handgunners cover the assault. The attackers are also using a cannon to blast holes in the stonework. More and more cannon were used in the 15th century to frighten defenders. Some siege guns were enormous.

PULLING YOUR WEIGHT
The traction trebuchet worked in the same way as the counterpoise version, except that the arm didn't bear a heavy weight but instead was moved by a team of men hauling on ropes. This meant that the machine was smaller than the counterpoise type and could not throw such large stones. But it could be reloaded more quickly. The sling was shorter, and a man held it out as the arm began to rise. He had to remember to let go!

OLD AND NEW
A trebuchet towers over a gunner and his small cannon in this early-15th-century picture.

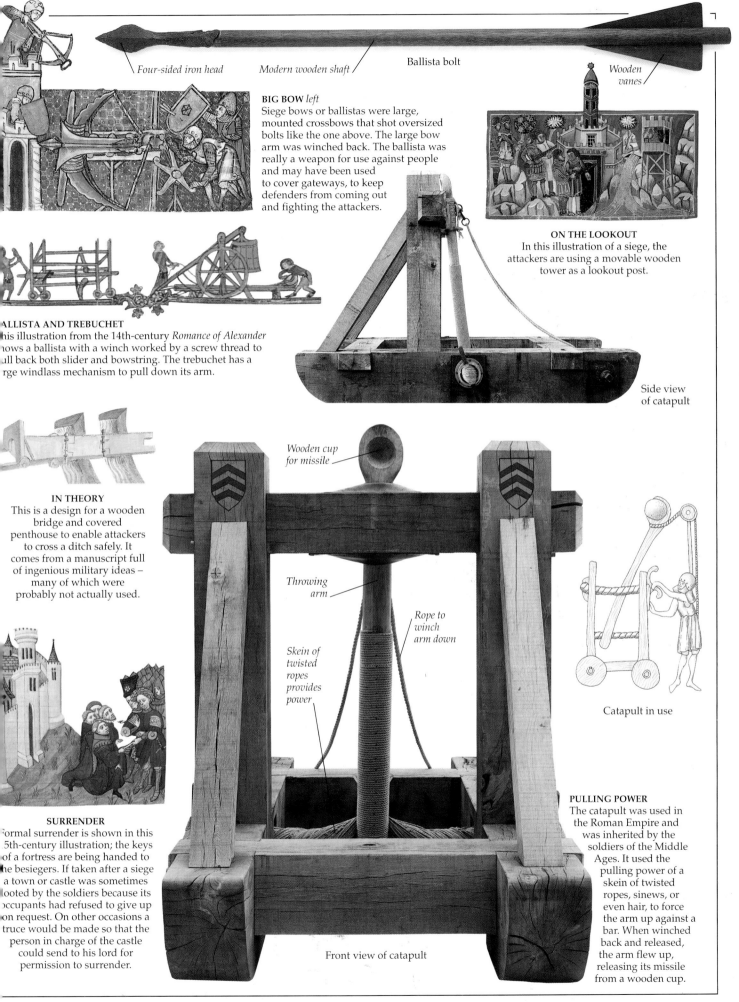

Four-sided iron head   *Modern wooden shaft*   Ballista bolt

Wooden vanes

BIG BOW *left*
Siege bows or ballistas were large, mounted crossbows that shot oversized bolts like the one above. The large bow arm was winched back. The ballista was really a weapon for use against people and may have been used to cover gateways, to keep defenders from coming out and fighting the attackers.

ON THE LOOKOUT
In this illustration of a siege, the attackers are using a movable wooden tower as a lookout post.

BALLISTA AND TREBUCHET
This illustration from the 14th-century *Romance of Alexander* shows a ballista with a winch worked by a screw thread to pull back both slider and bowstring. The trebuchet has a large windlass mechanism to pull down its arm.

Side view of catapult

IN THEORY
This is a design for a wooden bridge and covered penthouse to enable attackers to cross a ditch safely. It comes from a manuscript full of ingenious military ideas – many of which were probably not actually used.

Wooden cup for missile

Throwing arm

Rope to winch arm down

Skein of twisted ropes provides power

Catapult in use

SURRENDER
Formal surrender is shown in this 15th-century illustration; the keys of a fortress are being handed to the besiegers. If taken after a siege a town or castle was sometimes looted by the soldiers because its occupants had refused to give up on request. On other occasions a truce would be made so that the person in charge of the castle could send to his lord for permission to surrender.

Front view of catapult

PULLING POWER
The catapult was used in the Roman Empire and was inherited by the soldiers of the Middle Ages. It used the pulling power of a skein of twisted ropes, sinews, or even hair, to force the arm up against a bar. When winched back and released, the arm flew up, releasing its missile from a wooden cup.

Arming for the fight

E ARLY ARMOR was quite easy to put on. Mail was pulled on over the head, and a coat of plates (pp. 12–13) was buckled at the back, or at the sides and shoulders. Plate armor was more tricky to put on, but a knight could be armed by his squire in a few minutes and the armor could be speedily removed if necessary. After putting on a garment called an arming doublet, a knight was always armed from the feet upward, finishing with the helmet. In the 15th century, certain pieces of armor were laced to the arming doublet, but in the following century these pieces were more often attached to each other by straps or rivets. Here a squire is arming a knight in late-15th-century German "Gothic" style armor.

Mail gusset

Arming doublet

Waxed points

1 ARMING DOUBLET
This padded garment has waxed thongs (called points) to fasten different parts of the armor. Therefore the armor cannot be put on without the arming doublet. The mail gussets on the doublet are under the gaps that will be left by the plates.

Cuis

Pole

Grea

Sabato

2 SABATON, GREAVE, POLEYN, AND CUISSE
The sabaton and greave, for foot and lower leg, are followed by the poleyn, which is attached to the cuisse. The top edge is laced up to the torso.

3 MAIL SKIRT
Mail is secured around the waist to protect the groin, another area not fully covered by the plates. Using flexible mail here makes it easier to bend or sit.

Backplate

Flanged edge

4 BACKPLATE
The backplate is placed in position. It has a flanged lower edge to deflect weapons from the buttocks and legs. A strap and buckle are riveted to the lower front edges.

Breast- plate

Wai stra

5 BREASTPLATE
Breast and back together are called the cuirass. They are held together by the waist straps and are also connected at the shoulders.

Pauldron

Besague

Vambrace

Vambrace

Couter

Leather
glove inside
gauntlet

Rondel
dagger

Sword

Sword belt

7 GAUNTLETS, SWORD, AND DAGGER
The gauntlets are fitted with a leather glove to allow the knight to grip his weapons. His sword belt has straps to hold the scabbard at a convenient angle. A rondel dagger hangs at his right side.

PAULDRON, COUTER, VAMBRACE, AND BESAGUE
The upper arm guard (vambrace) and elbow piece (couter) are tied by laces through pairs of holes in the plates. The pauldron and besague guard the knight's shoulder and armpit.

ARMING A KNIGHT
A rare picture of about 1450 shows a knight being armed for foot combat in the lists. His arming doublet can be seen.

10 FULLY ARMED
The knight holds a mace, which is an effective weapon against plate armor. Armed from head to foot (or cap-a-pie) he is now ready to mount his warhorse.

Bevor

Helmet

Mace

BEVOR
A "bevor," or chin defense, is added to protect the lower half of the face when wearing the sallet, a form of helmet especially popular in Germany.

Rowel spur

9 SPURS AND HELMET
The knight's rowel spurs (pp. 20–21) are buckled to his feet; the helmet, lined inside for comfort and to cushion blows, is placed on his head. The helmet has a chin strap to keep it from being knocked off in combat.

29

The enemy

Knights soon found themselves facing infantry capable of defeating them. The English axmen at Hastings in 1066 cut down Norman knights, while Flemish footsoldiers with clubs defeated French horsemen at Courtrai in 1302. Massed Scottish spear formations stopped cavalry charges at Bannockburn in 1314. The Swiss favored the same tactic but used pikes. Different types of bow were highly effective against mounted knights. English longbowmen broke up cavalry charges by French knights at Crécy in 1346 and dismounted knights at Agincourt in 1415. The lethal crossbow shot short bolts from increasingly powerful weapons. In 15th-century Bohemia (now part of the Czech lands) the Hussites blasted German knights, using the first massed guns, fired from the protection of wagons.

THE LONGBOW
This type of bow was usually made of a stave of yew wood about the height of the archer himself. It was usually fitted with horn nocks at the tips to take the hemp string. War bows probably needed a pull of at least 80 lb (36 kg) and many may have been far more powerful.

Barbed arrow-head

Leather bracer

Stave of yew wood

Horn nock to take string

Arrows stood in front for quick reloading

SLINGER
Some lightly armed infantrymen used slings. The stone or lead pellets were lethal if they struck someone in the face, and groups of slingers could force defenders to keep their heads down during sieges. However, they could not damage armor. Sometimes a sling was attached to a wooden handle to increase range; this device was called a staff sling.

A BRISTLING HEDGE
Cavalrymen were unhappy about forcing their horses against spears, and infantry in close formation with a "hedge" of spears could hold off mounted knights. It then became necessary for archers to try and break up the formations by shooting missiles. The pike was even longer and more effective.

AN ARCHER
Longbows were used in many European countries, although on the mainland the crossbow was much more popular. The English used large numbers of archers, notably against the French during the Hundred Years War in the 14th and 15th centuries. In drawing a longbow the string was brought back somewhere between the cheek and the ear. The leather bracer protected the arms from an accidental slap from the string; a leather tab protected the drawer's fingers. Archers wore various pieces of defensive armor, or just a simple padded doublet, as here.

AT THE BUTTS
The strength required to pull a longbow meant that archers
needed constant practice to keep in condition and maintain
their skills. In this 14th-century picture English archers
shoot at the butts, targets set up on earthen mounds.

THE GOOSE FEATHER
Fletchings, or feather flights, make the arrow spin for a truer
flight. Usually goose feathers were used for the vast numbers of
arrows needed by an army. The shaft was commonly made
from ash wood. The nock holds the arrow lightly on the string.

Nock inset
into shaft

Goose feather

Binding

Bodkin

LONG-RANGE FIGHTING
Arrows from a longbow
would probably fly about
1000 ft (300 m), which
meant that a "creeping
barrage" of
arrows could be
dropped on an
advancing enemy.
This was done by shooting
the arrows upward.
Cavalry horses were
especially vulnerable –
some part of the horse
was always unprotected
and became
uncontrollable when
wounded. Bodkins could
punch through mail links.

*Fragment
of shaft*

General-purpose

Bodkin

Bodkin

General-purpose

Broadhead

ARROWHEADS
These varied in shape depending on their use.
Broadheads were barbed for use against
animals; some were used against warhorses.
Bodkins were for penetrating armor. A thin
bodkin could pierce armor plate when it struck
its target squarely. There were also general-
purpose arrowheads.

*Arrow
through belt*

*Steel buckler
or fist shield*

WELSH ARCHER
The English came up against
Welsh longbowmen in the
12th century, and such men
were often employed in English
armies afterward. In this crude
picture the rough bow is shown
far too small. The bare foot may
be to give a better grip.

*Pieces of leg
armor for
partial protection*

LONGBOW VERSUS CROSSBOW
A skilled archer might release 12 arrows per minute. A
crossbowman, using a windlass (mechanical winder), could only
shoot two bolts in the same time. But these would penetrate
deeply, and the crossbowman did not need so much training. In
this late-15th-century illustration the crossbowman uses a
windlass to pull back a powerful steel bow arm.

KEEN EYE
Each archer carried 24 arrows,
known as a sheaf, and when
these were shot away more were
brought from supply wagons.
Many archers carried their
arrows pushed through their
belt rather than in a quiver,
which was also usually hung
from the waist. They would
often stick their arrows into the
ground in front of them, ready
for quick shooting.

Into battle

WARRIOR KINGS
The great seals of many medieval kings showed them as head of their army, on horseback, and wearing full armor. Nobles also liked to portray themselves in this way. Here Henry I, king of England (1100–1135) and duke of Normandy, wears a mail coat and conical helmet.

THE RULES OF CHIVALRY dictated that knights should show courtesy to defeated enemies. This was not just humane, it brought ransoms from high-ranking prisoners. But this code was not always observed, especially by desperate men facing death. For example, English longbowmen supported by knights slaughtered French knights at the battles of Crécy (1346), Poitiers (1356), and Agincourt (1415). And knights often showed little mercy to foot soldiers, cutting them down ruthlessly in pursuit. Much was at stake in a battle; defeat might mean the loss of an army or even a throne. So commanders preferred to ravage and raid enemy territory. This brought extra supplies as well as destroying property, and showed that the local lord could not protect his people in turn. Keeping troops close to an enemy's army kept it from ravaging in turn.

FIGHTING ON FOOT
Although knights were trained as horsemen, they did not always go into battle as cavalrymen. On many occasions it was thought better for a large part of an army to dismount and form a solid body, often supported by archers and groups of cavalry. In this late-14th-century illustration, dismounted English and French knights and men-at-arms, many wearing visored basinets on their heads (pp. 12–13), clash on a bridge. Archers and crossbowmen assist them.

CALTROPS
These nasty-looking iron objects are only a couple of inches high. They were scattered over the ground before a battle to lame horses or men from the opposing army who accidentally stepped on them. However they fell, caltrops always landed with one spike pointing upward. They were also scattered in front of castles.

IN PURSUIT
A mid-13th-century battle scene shows the point when one force in the battle has turned in flight and is pursued by the other side. Often the pursuers did not hesitate to strike at men with their backs turned, and once a man was down, his opponent would give him several further cuts to make sure he stayed there. Breaking ranks to chase the enemy could sometimes put the rest of your army in danger.

WALL OF HORSES *above*

Armor of the 12th century was similar in many parts of Europe, but fighting methods could vary. Instead of using their lances to stab overhand or even to throw, as sometimes happened in the 11th century, the Italian knights on this stone carving are "couching" – tucking – them under their arms. Each side charges in close formation, hoping to steamroller over their opponents.

SHOCK OF BATTLE
This late-15th-century picture shows the crash of two opposing cavalry forces in full plate armor and the deadly effects of well-aimed lances. Those struck down in the first line, even if only slightly wounded, were liable to be trampled by the horses either of the enemy or of their own knights following behind.

SPOILS OF WAR
When an army was defeated the victors would often capture the baggage. This could contain many valuables, especially if the losing leader was a prince. Captured towns also provided rich pickings, and prisoners and dead knights were stripped of their armor after a battle. In this 14th-century Italian picture the victors examine the spoils.

SHOCK WAVES
This early-16th-century German woodcut shows a disciplined charge by mounted knights. Spurring their horses to a gallop as they near the enemy, the first line has made contact while those behind follow with lances still raised. They will lower their lances before meeting their opponents.

ne spike always
ints upward

Three spikes rest on the ground

The castle at peace

THE CASTLE DID NOT JUST house a garrison – it was home for the knight and his household. The most important building inside the castle was the great hall, where everyone ate meals, and day-to-day business was done. Sometimes there were private rooms for the lord. There was also a kitchen (often outdoors because of the danger of fire), a chapel, armorer's workshop, blacksmith, stables, kennels, pens for animals, and large storerooms to keep the castle well stocked. A water supply was vital; a well, usable in times of siege, was preferred. Outer walls might be whitewashed to protect against the weather; inner walls could be plastered and painted in attractive colors. Castles were useful resting places for nobles who were traveling. When they were expected, the rooms were made ready and the floors might be covered with fresh straw, rushes, or sweet-smelling grasses.

SONG AND DANCE
Music was welcomed as entertainment and to accompany meals. Dances usually involved many people, often holding hands for types of ring dance.

Coat-of-arms

WALL SCONCE
Only the rich could afford wax candles burn in sconces like this 16th-century French example. Made of gilt copper, i bears the coat-of-arms of the Castelnau LaLoubere family encircled by the collar the Order of St. Michael.

SILVER CRUET
This silver vessel was kept in the chapel to hold the holy water or wine used in the Mass. It was made in Burgundy in the late 14th century.

AT THE LORD'S TABLE
At mealtimes the whole household would come together in the great hall. On this manuscript of about 1316, Lancelot entertains King Arthur by telling him about his adventures.

BLAZING FIRE
Large fireplaces could be set in the thick stone walls of castles. The woman is spinning woolen thread (pp. 38–39).

Limoges enamel decoration

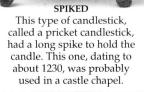

SPIKED
This type of candlestick, called a pricket candlestick, had a long spike to hold the candle. This one, dating to about 1230, was probably used in a castle chapel.

A GAME OF CHESS
King Francis I of France plays chess with Margaret of Angoulême in a picture of about 1504. Being a war game, chess was popular with knights Chess pieces were often made of beautifully carved bone or ivory.

inted and tooled
ather sheath

HAND BASIN
Pairs of basins like this, called gemellions, were used to wash peoples' hands at the table. A servant would pour water over the person's hands from one basin into the other and then dry the hands with a towel. Sometimes the water was poured from a ewer (pitcher) instead. This gemellion is decorated with Limoges enamels.

Household musician

A knight kneels before his lady

SERVING KNIVES
Pairs of broad-bladed knives like these 15th-century
rman ones were used for serving food. Each handle is
ounted in brass and the grips have mahogany panels
vith plaques of stag horn. Each blade has an ancient
wastika symbol. The leather sheath has lost its cap.

Y THE GAME
rd games helped to
s long evenings.
re a young man of
early 14th century
ys checkers with a
y. Backgammon
s also popular.

CHAMBER POT
Richer people might use chamber pots, like this one, for convenience, although castles often had lavatories built into the walls. These consisted of a seat connected to a shute which opened directly on to the outside of the castle wall.

lyard
ght

BRONZE WEIGHTS
The late-13th-century steelyard weight was hung from a pivoting metal arm to figure out the weight of an object placed on the other end. The weight on the right has the English royal arms in the version used after 1405.

Royal arms

The lord of the manor

SOME KNIGHTS were mercenary soldiers who fought simply for money. Others, particularly until the 13th century, lived at their lord's expense as household troops in his castle. But a man might be given some land by his lord. Then he became lord of the manor and lived off its produce. He lived in a manor house, often of stone and with its own defenses. He held a large part of the manor as the home farm; "his" peasants, workers of varying status, owed him service in return for their homes. They had to bake their bread in his oven and pay for the privilege. Both the lord and the church received part of their goods, although they might be invited to feasts at festivals, such as Lammas (when bread made from the season's first corn was blessed). The lord sat in judgment in the manor court and might have a house in a town for business dealings.

HOME DEFENSE
Stokesay is a fortified manor house in Shropshire, England. It consists of a hall and chamber block with a tower at each end, mostly built in the late 13th century. In the 17th century a wooden section was added on one end.

Original

MY SEAL ON IT
Noblemen often could not read or write. Instead of signing a document they added a wax seal, pressed fr a metal die. This is the silver seal die, with a modern cas of Robert Fitzwalter, one of the leaders of the rebel Englis barons who made King John sign the Magna Carta in 1215.

ALL IN THE GAME
This wealthy 14th-century Italian couple whiles away the time with a board game. Knights' only other entertainment came from resident or strolling players, musicians, or poets.

Modern cast

Name of Robert Fitzwalter, owner of the seal

IVORY CHESS PIEC
These Scandinavian chessm found on the Isle of Lev Scotland, are carved fr walrus ivory and date fr the mid-12th centu

Queen

King

Bishop

Knight

Warder (Rook)

UPHILL STRUGGLE

The medieval peasant had a life of hard work in the fields, sowing and harvesting the crops. The 14th-century Luttrell Psalter shows peasants trying to max a hay cart up a steep slope.

GARDEN OF DELIGHT

One of the houses on this 15th-century manor is made of a framework of timbers filled in with wattle and daub (twigs and mud), and then whitewashed. Close by is an orchard of fruit trees.

LIKE FATHER, LIKE SON

These details from an altar cloth of about 1500 show a knight in prayer, with his seven sons. Large families were common. The eldest son would follow his father and become a knight (pp. 10–11). Daughters would hope to marry noblemen (pp. 38–39). Younger children often became priests or nuns.

DECORATED CASKET

This large box belonged to a rich family of the early 15th century. It is made of wood covered in bone panels carved with biblical scenes from the story of Susanna and the Elders.

THE LORD

The status and rank of a lord varied, as did the size of his manor. Some lords were powerful men who held a number of manors, visiting them as necessary. A bailiff would look after the running of the estates when the lord was away. He might go on trips to a town where merchants carried on their trade and where lords in need of money could borrow it from money-lenders.

The lady of the manor

THE LIFE OF THE LADY
The lady ruled the domestic areas – the kitchens and living quarters – of the castle or manor house. She had officials to run the houshold affairs, but she had to check the accounts and agree to any expenses. It was her duty to receive guests courteously and arrange for their accommodation. Ladies-in-waiting were her companions; maidservants attended her; and nurses looked after her children. The children were very important, for the lady's main role in medieval society was to provide heirs.

W OMEN IN THE MIDDLE AGES, even those of noble rank, had far fewer rights than a woman can expect today. Young women were often married by the age of 14. A girl's family would arrange her marriage and she would be given a dowry, a gift to pass on to her husband. Upon marriage a woman's inheritance passed to the husband, so knights were often on the lookout for a rich heiress to marry. But the lady was her husband' equal in private life. She could provide great support for him and take responsibility for the castle when he was away. She might even have to defend the castle if it was besieged, and hol it against her enemies.

DALLIANCE
The ideal of courtly love is shown in an illustration from the medieval poem *The Romance of the Rose*. Women pass the time pleasantly, listening to a song while a fountain pours water into an ornamental stream. In reality, many women would not have had time for such activities.

THE WHITE SWAN
This gold-and-enamel brooch is known as the Dunstable Swan and dates from the early 15th century. The swan was used as a badge by the House of Lancaster (one of the English ruling families), particularly by the princes of Wales. Noblewomen might wear such badges to show their allegiance.

BAD NEWS
A lady swoons on receiving news of her husband's death. Although marriages were arranged by the couple's families, husband and wife could and did become extremely fond of one another and sometimes grew to love each other.

Flemish gold brooch

JEWELS
Women liked to diplay their rank by wearing rings and brooches. The 15th-century gold brooch at the top is probably Flemish and has a female figure among the precious stones. The late-14th-century English brooch is decorated with coiled monsters.

English gold brooch

WOMEN OF ACCOMPLISHMENT
Ladies were often very well educated. Some could read and write, understand Latin, and speak foreign languages. In this picture of the 1460s, learned ladies with books represent Philosphy and the Liberal Arts.

ON BENDED KNEE
A knight of about 1200 places his hands in those of his lady in an act of homage like that performed by a subordinate to his lord. In this case he is indicating that he will be his lady's servant – an ideal of courtly love that was not borne out in practice.

MERCI

"SUITABLE" OCCUPATIONS
Women were expected to know how to spin wool, but some men thought teaching them to read was dangerous. In this early-15th-century picture one woman spins woolen thread while another cards, or combs out, the wool.

Pommel

Cantle

SIDESADDLE
Noblewomen were often active hunters. This medallion of 1477 shows Mary of Burgundy. She carries her hawk on her wrist and is riding sidesaddle, a method that solved the difficulty of sitting on a horse in a long dress. Her mount wears a decorative cloth trapper.

TALE ON A SADDLE
This German saddle dates from between about 1440 and 1480. It is made of wood covered with plaques of stag's horn, on which are carved the figures of a man and a woman repeated several times. Inlaid hard wax provides the color. The figures' speech is written on scrolls. They speak of their love and of the woman's husband's absence in the war; the woman asks: "But if the war should end?"

Carved plaque

The ideal of chivalry

ALTHOUGH KNIGHTS were men of war, they traditionally behaved in a courteous and civil way when dealing with their enemies. In the 12th century this kind of behavior was extended to form a knightly code of conduct, with a special emphasis on courtly manners toward women. The poems of courtly love recited by the troubadours of southern France were based on this code, and the romance stories that became popular in the 13th century showed the ways a warrior should behave. Churchmen liked the idea of high standards and made the knighting ceremony a religious occasion with a church vigil and purifying bath (pp. 10–11). Books on chivalry also appeared, though in reality knights often found it difficult to live up to the ideal.

GEORGE AND THE DRAGON
St. George was a soldier martyred (put to death because of his religion) by the Romans in about A.D. 350. During the Middle Ages stories appeared telling how he rescued a king's daughter from a dragon. He became especially connected with England. This carved ivory shows St. George with the battlements of a castle in the background.

KNIGHT IN SHINING ARMOR
This 15th-century tournament parade shield depicts a bareheaded knight kneeling before his lady. The words on the scroll mean "You or death," and the figure of death is represented by a skeleton.

TRUE-LOVE KNOTS
Medallions like this were sometimes made to mark special occasions, such as marriages. This one was struck to comemorate the marriage of Margaret of Austria to the Duke of Savoy in 1502. The knots in the background are the badge of Savoy – they also refer to the way the couple's love will unite the two families.

WHAT'S IN A NAME?
This scene, from the 15th-century book *The Lovelorn Heart*, by Frenchman René of Anjou, illustrates the strange world of the medieval romance in which people can stand for objects or feelings. Here the knight, called Cueur (meaning Heart), reads an inscription while his companion, Desire, lies sleeping.

LANCELOT AND GUINEVERE
King Arthur was probably a fifth-century warrior, but the legends of the king and the knights of the Round Table gained popularity in 13th-century Europe. They tell of Arthur's struggles against evil and of the love between Arthur's queen, Guinevere, and Sir Lancelot, which eventually led to the destruction of Arthur's court. In this story, Lancelot crosses a sword bridge to rescue Guinevere.

THE KNIGHT OF THE CART
Knights rode on horseback and it was usually thought a disgrace for a knight to travel in a cart. This picture shows an episode from the story of Sir Lancelot. Lancelot was famous for his valour and skill in combat, but his love affair with Queen Guinevere brought him shame. In this episode Lancelot meets a dwarf who offers to tell him where Guinevere is if he will ride in the cart.

ROYAL CHAMPION
Sir Edward Dymoke was the champion of Queen Elizabeth I. At her coronation banquet in Westminster, it was his job to ride fully armed into the hall and hurl his gauntlet to the ground to defy anyone who wished to question the queen's right to rule. Such a challenge was made at every English coronation until that of George IV in 1821.

Lock

Corner reinforcement

TRAGIC LOVERS
The ivory carvings on this 12th-century box show episodes from the story of Tristan and Iseult. This is a tale of the knight Tristan, who accidentally drank a love potion and fell in love with Iseult, the bride of his uncle, King Mark.

The tournament

FIGHTING MEN HAVE ALWAYS TRAINED for battle. Tournaments started, as practic for war, probably in the 11th century. Two teams of knights would fight a mock battle, called a tourney or mêlée, over a huge area of countryside, sometimes even assisted by foot soldiers. Defeated knights gave up their hors and armor to the victor, so a good fighter could make a fortune. At first, battle armor and sharp weapons were used, but blunted weapons were introduced the 13th century. Other contests, such as jousts (pp. 44–45) and combat on foo (pp. 46–47), also were held. In the *pas d'armes*, popular in the 15th century, one or more contestants held the lists, or tournament ground, and sent challenges to other knights and squires. In the 17th century the tournament was replaced in most countries by displays of horsemanship called carousels.

"Roped" comb

BIRD MEN ON PARAD
In the early 16th century it became fashionable wear helmets with strange mask-like visors the parades during tournaments. Sometim knights even wore them during the tourn itself. The visors were fitted otherwise normal close-helm (pp. 14–15). This one is like eagle's head, w feathers etch into the met

Eagle's be

Breaths for ventilation

WITH BANNERS FLYING
The colorful array of banners at a tournament was ideal for the display of coats of arms and all kinds of other fanciful designs. The knights also wore large crests on their helms, even when these were no longer worn in battle.

Devil

DEVIL TAKE YOU
Although tournaments were popular with knights, and many people liked to watch, the church frowned on them because much blood was often spilled. In this early-14th-century picture, devils wait to seize the souls of knights killed in a tourney.

A KNIGHT DISGRACED
The women viewed the banners and crested helms of the contestants before the tourney. If lady knew that one of the knight had done wrong, his helm was taken down and he was banned from the lists. This picture comes from the 15th-century tournamer book of Reúé of Anjou

CLUB TOURNEY

In a club tourney, two teams using blunt swords and clubs tried to knock the crests off their opponents' helmets, which were fitted with protective face grilles. Each knight had a banner-bearer, and attendants (called varlets) stood ready in case the knight fell. In this picture, the knight of honor rides between two ropes that separate the teams; ladies and judges are in the stands. The lists were small, but the artist has compressed everything to fit the picture.

Hole to take lance

Etched and gilt decoration

Plume holder

Face embossed in metal

Vamplate

VAMPLATE AND LOCKING-GAUNTLET

The circular vamplate was fixed over the lance to guard the knight's hand. Once the knight had gripped his sword the locking-gauntlet was locked shut so the sword was not lost in combat. It became popular in the 16th century. Both objects are from an Italian armor of about 1570.

PARADE CASQUE

This Italian open helmet of about 1530 was worn in parades. It has embossed decoration and the face has been given a plate shaped like teeth. It may once have had a lower set of teeth as well. The hinged earpieces are missing.

Metal plate imitating teeth

Neck guard

Locking-gauntlet

The joust

DURING THE 13TH CENTURY a dramatic new element was added to the tournament – jousts, in which knights fought one-on-one. In a joust, a knight could show his skill without other contestants getting in the way. Usually the knights fought on horseback with lances, though in some contests they continued the fight with swords. Two knights would charge toward each other at top speed and try to unhorse each other with a single blow of the lance. You could also score points if you broke your lance on your opponent's shield. In "jousts of war" knights used sharp lances. These could kill a knight, so many jousters preferred "jousts of peace," using a lance fitted with a blunt tip or with a "coronel" shaped like a small crown to spread the impact. Special armor was developed for jousting, to increase protection. A barrier called the tilt was introduced in the 15th century to separate the knights and avoid collisions.

Eye slit

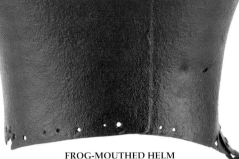

FROG-MOUTHED HELM
This 15th-century helmet for the jousts of peace was originally fastened down the back and front. The wearer could see his opponent by leaning forward during the charge. At the moment of impact he straightened up, so that the "frog-mouthed" lower lip protected his eyes from the lance head or fragments of the shaft.

Curved edge to support lance

GERMANIC JOUSTERS
In the Germanic countries, knights often practised the *Rennen*, a version of the jousts of war. As no barrier was used, the knights' legs were partially protected by metal shields.

LANCER'S SHIELD
This late 15th-century wooden shield is covered in leather. It was probably used for the *Rennen*. The lance could be placed in the recess in the side. The shield was attached to the breastplate by a staple nailed to the rear.

BREAKING A LANCE
Lances were made of wood and by the 16th century were often fluted to help them splinter easily. This 17th-century lance is slightly thinner than those used for jousting against an opponent. It was used to spear a small ring hanging from a bracket.

PARADE BEFORE THE TILT
Knights paraded beside the tilt, or barrier, before the jousting commenced. This scene from Jean Froissart's *Chronicles* was painted in the late 15th century, though it depicts the jousts at St. Inglevert, which took place in 1390, before the tilt was introduced. Attendants with spare lances accompany the knights

Knights took part in many different types of combat, so armors were sometimes supplied with additional pieces to allow them to be assembled in various ways. The reinforcing pieces shown here are from South Germany and were made in about 1550. They are for a version of the jousts of peace known as the "tilt in the Italian fashion." Extra protection is provided mainly for the left side of the body, because the knights passed one another on that side. Knights did not need great maneuverability when jousting, so rigid extra pieces could be bolted on. These were often heavier or thicker pieces than those used on field armor. So jousting armor was heavy and difficult to move around in, but this did not matter, because such armour did not have to be worn for long periods, and safety was a priority.

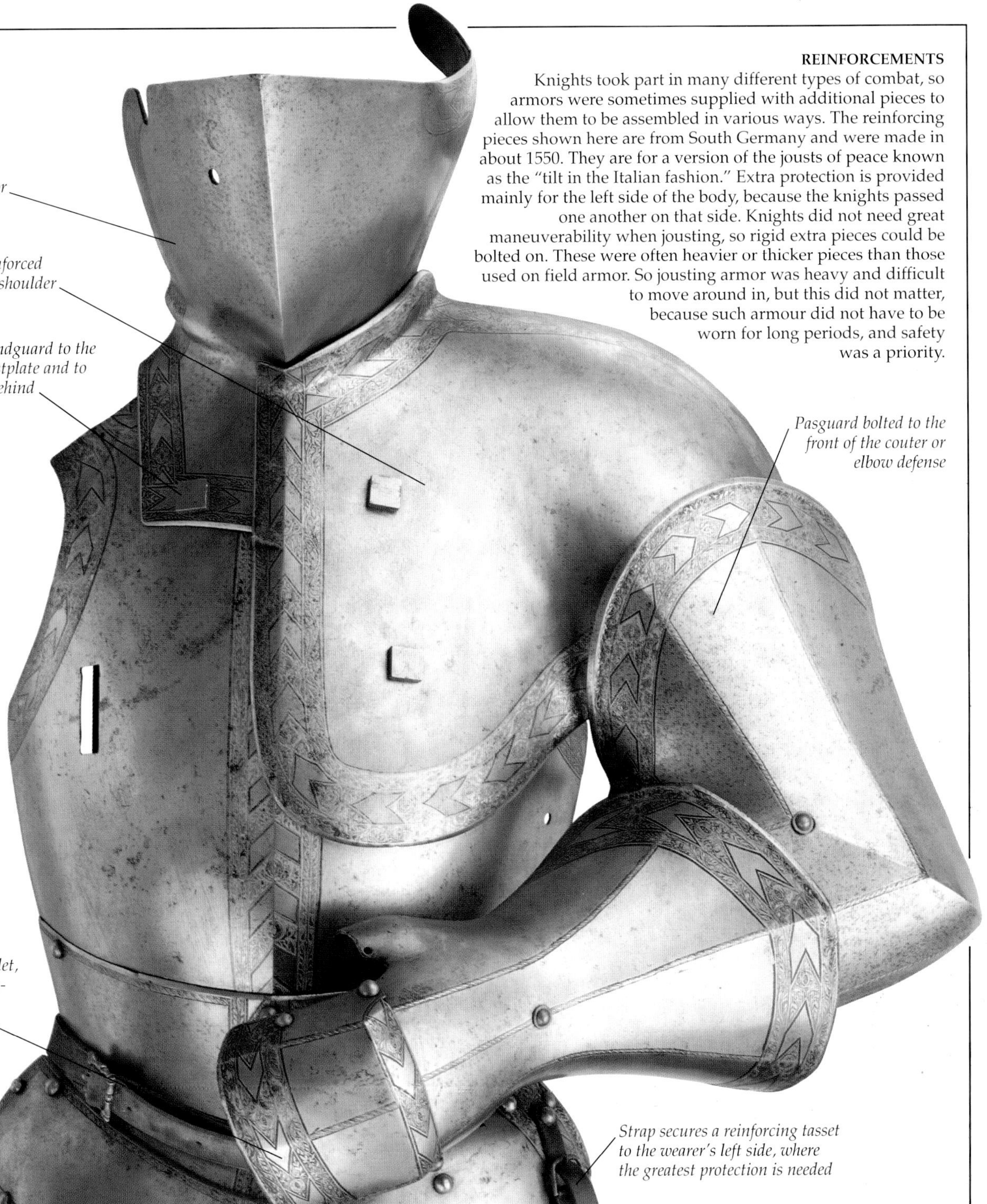

Reinforcing bevor

Grandguard reinforced the wearer's left shoulder

Bolt joining grandguard to the reinforcing breastplate and to the breastplate behind

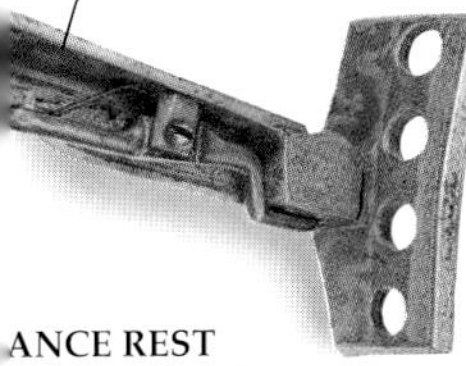

Protruding arm to support lance

LANCE REST

This was fixed to the breastplate by staples. It helped to hold the weight of the lance and kept it from sliding back through the armpit on impact.

Large reinforcing gauntlet, here with flexible mitten-style finger plates

Pasguard bolted to the front of the couter or elbow defense

Strap secures a reinforcing tasset to the wearer's left side, where the greatest protection is needed

Reinforcing tasset

WATERY WARRIORS

A version of the joust was sometimes carried out on water, as this early-14th-century miniature shows. Two teams of rowers propelled their boats toward one another while a man in the prow of each tried to knock his opponent off balance.

OLD-STYLE JOUSTING

These 15th-century knights are jousting in the old style, without a barrier. This style remained especially popular in the German countries. The knights' lances are fitted with coronels and are placed in the shield recesses.

Foot combat

In some 13th-century jousts the knights dismounted after using their lances and continued fighting with swords. By the 14th century, such foot combats were popular in their own right. Contestants took turns delivering blows, and men-at-arms stood ready to separate fighters who got too excited. From 15th-century writings we learn that each man sometimes threw a javelin first, then fought with sword, ax, or staff weapon. Later still, such combats were replaced by contests in which two teams fought across a barrier. These contests were called foot tournaments because, as in the mounted tourney (pp. 42–43), each man tried to break a spear against his opponent before continuing the fight with blunted swords.

AT THE READY
This detail from a 16th-century Flemish tapestry shows contestants waiting to take part in foot combat over the barrier. A page is handing one knight his helmet.

Sword cuts

Visor

Holes for lace of cross straps hold th head inside

Chin piece

CLOSE-HELME
This helmet was designed f the tournament on foot. It is so rich gilded that it is surprising that it was ev worn in actual combat. But the sword cuts sho that it must have been used. It was part of dazzling garniture of gilt armor made in 155

FORMAL FIGHT
Foot combats in the 15th century took place without a barrier, so the contestants protected their legs with armor. The most common helmet for these contests was the great basinet (pp. 12–13), which was outdated for war by the middle of the century.

Hand-threaded screw

BROW REINFORCE
This plate was screwed to the visor of the close-helmet shown on the right. It gave more protection to the left side of the head.

Hole for hearing

Visor

Bevor

Eyeslit

EXCHANGE VISOR
Two threaded bolts allowed the visor to be removed from the helmet on the left and replaced with this one, which has a number of ventilation holes. It could be used for battle or for foot combat.

Lifting peg

Pivoting fork for holding up bevor

ARMET
In this type of helmet the cheek-pieces pivot outward when it is put on, instead of the front half of the helmet swinging up as in the helmet at top right. This German example of about 1535 has a visor that fits inside the rim of the bevor, where it is held by a spring-catch. The bevor is locked over the cheek piece in the same way.

TRIAL BY BATTLE
Not all foot contests were held for sport. Sometimes a charge of murder or treason was settled by a combat, in which God was thought to help the innocent man. The contest went on until one was either killed or surrendered, in which case he was executed.

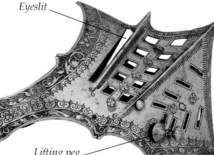

POLE-AX

This weapon was very popular in battle and foot combat. It was used to strike the opponent's head (the word "poll" meant head) and the solid hammer-head at the back could concuss a man in armor. The long langets of this example of about 1470 helped to hold the head firmly and keep the shaft from being cut in combat.

FOOT-COMBAT ARMOR

This German armor of about 1580 forms part of a garniture, or collection of pieces. Some larger garnitures could be made into several different armors. The surface was originally blued, and is etched and gilded, with the ornament outlined in black. The visor and upper bevor lock together with a bolt. This keeps them from accidentally flying open if struck, a safety feature of some foot-combat helmets. No leg armor was worn because the combat took place over a barrier and blows below this level were forbidden.

Plate to deflect side blows from the head

Pauldron

Langet

Rondel protects the hand

Gauntlet

THE BARRIER
This crude drawing of the late 16th century shows knights taking part in a foot contest over the barrier.

Heraldry

Or, a pale gules

Azure, a fess embattled or

Sable, a cross engrailed or

Lozengy, argent and gules

Vert, a crescent or

Azure, a fleur- de-lys or

Gules, a spur argent

Mᴇɴ ʜᴀᴠᴇ ᴀʟᴡᴀʏs decorated their shields. In the 12th century these designs became more standardized in a system known as heraldry, which enabled a knight to be identified by symbols on his shield, or a full coat of arms. It is often said that this was done because helmets with face guards made knights difficult to recognize, but a more likely reason was the need to identify contestants in tournaments. Heraldry was based on strict rules. Only one coat of arms was carried by a knight, and this passed to his eldest son when he died. Other children used variants of their father's arms. Arms used a series of standard colors and "metals" (silver or gold) and are described in a special language, based on Old French.

BADGE OF OFFICE
This copper arm badge was worn by a servant of François de Lorraine, Hospitaler Prior of France from 1549 to 1563, whose arms it bears. Retainers of a lord often wore his livery badge.

COSTUME DESIGN
The fleur-de-lys, heraldic emblem of France, is used to decorate this long tunic. The fur lining of the mantle was also adapted for heraldic purposes.

ROLL OF ARMS
Heralds made lists to keep a record of participants in military events like tournaments and battles. The Carlisle Roll contains 277 shields of King Edward III's retinue on his visit to Carlisle, England, in 1334.

HERALDIC JAR
Coats of arms were placed on all sorts of objects, to show ownership or simply to add color. This jar of about 1500 has quartered arms, in which the arms of two families joined by marriage appear twice together.

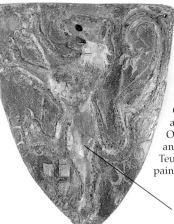

A KNIGHT'S SHIELD
This rare surviving shield of the 13th century is made from wood, which has a lion rampant moulded in leather. These are the arms of a landgrave (ruler) of Hesse in Germany. He is represented as a knight of the Teutonic Order, as the white shield and black cross of the Teutonic knights has been painted on the lower left.

Lion rampant

Arms of Cosimo de' Medici

ORD ARMS
is Italian falchion,
short cutting
ord, dates from the
d-16th century. It is
ned with the arms
Cosimo I de'
dici, Duke of
rence. It is
ircled with the
ar of the Order
he Golden
ece, one of
eral knightly
lers of chivalry.

Pommel of gilt bronze cast in shape of a lion's head

COLORFUL SPECTACLE
In this 15th-century picture, shields of the knightly passengers are hung over the sides of boats, largely for display. Colorful heraldic banners bore the arms of their knightly owners and were a rallying point in battle, as were the longer standards, which carried a lord's badges and other devices. Here the French royal arms appear on trumpet banners.

Gules, a lion
rampant or

Or, a lion sejant
regardant purpure

MAKING AN IMPRESSION
The bezel of this large gold 14th-century signet ring is engraved with heraldic arms, which include those of the de Grailly family. Above are the letters: "EID Gre," probably meaning: "This is the seal of Jean de Grailly." When pressed into hot wax used to seal a document, the arms appeared in the wax the right way around.

Gules, a swan
argent

Azure, a dolphin
naiant argent

Or, a dragon
rampant vert

Or, a portcullis
purpure

COAT OF ARMS
The brass of Sir Thomas
nerhasset (died 1531) shows
e heraldic arms on his coat
mor, the name given to the
rcoat. The version worn at
his time is the tabard, also
used by heralds.

SPANISH PLATE
The Spanish kingdom of Castile had a castle for its arms, while that of Leon used a lion. These are the earliest "quartered arms," first noted in 1272. On this Spanish dish of about 1425 the true heraldic colors have been ignored, while the background has designs influenced by the Spanish Muslims.

KEY TO LABELS ON ARMS

Or	Gold
Argent	Silver
Gules	Red
Azure	Blue
Sable	Black
Vert	Green
Purpure	Purple

Azure, a sun in
splendor or

Hunting and hawking

MEDIEVAL MONARCHS AND LORDS were very fond of hunting and hawking. These sports provided fresh meat, as well as helped to train knights for war. Hunting, for example, allowed them to show their courage when facing dangerous animals like a wild boar. The Norman kings set aside vast areas of woodland for hunting in England, and there were severe penalties for poachers or anyone who broke the forest laws. The animals hunted ranged from deer and boar to birds and rabbits. Knights often hunted on horseback, which provided excitement and useful practice for war. Sometimes "beaters" drove the prey toward the huntsmen, who lay in wait. Hunters might also use bows or crossbows, which gave them good experience with these weapons. Hawking was very popular, and good birds were prized. One 15th-century manuscript gives a list of hawks, showing how only the higher members of society could fly the best birds.

FLYING TO A LU...
A lure was a dumm... bird which the falco... swung from a lo... cord. The falcon wou... pounce on the lure, ... that the falconer co... retrieve ... bird. The lu... could also ... used to ex... cise a bird ... teach it to cli... high and "stoop... dive – down ... its pr...

Steel pin to engage rack drawing bow

NOBLE BEASTS
This detail of the carving on the side of the crossbow tiller shows a stag hunt. Only rich people were allowed to hunt stags.

Wooden tiller veneered with polished stag horn carved in relief

Wooden flights

WOODEN FEATHERS
These German crossbow bolts date to about 1470. One has wooden flights rather than the feathers usually seen on arrows.

FOR DEER HUNTERS *below*
The blade of a German hunting sword of about 1540 is etched with scenes of a stag hunt. Such swords were carried for hunting and also for general protection.

WOLF HUNT
When hunting for wolves, huntsmen would hang pieces of meat in a thicket and drag them along pathways to leave a scent. Look-outs in trees warned of the wolf's approach and mastiff dogs flushed it out for the hunters. This hunt is pictured in a copy of the late-14th-century hunting book of Gaston Phoebus, Count of Foix, France.

FREDERICK II THE FALCONER
This German emperor liked falconry so much th... in the mid-13th century he wrote a book on th... subject, from which this picture comes. Some lor... even kept hawks in their private rooms.

Deer being driven into nets

Dogs chasing the deer

Hunting horn

Man shooting squirrel

Falconer

ON THE HUNT
A Flemish or German silver plaque of about 1600 shows knights hunting with hounds, falconry, and guns. One hound catches a hare in front of three ladies who watch with interest from their carriage.

Revolving nut released by trigger below

Triangular barbed head

PET CARE
...nting dogs needed ...reful looking after. ...Gaston Phoebus ...commends the use ...f herbal medicines ...to cure mange, ...diseases of the eye, ...ar, and throat, and ...en rabies. Swollen ...paws damaged by ...ny plants required ...tention. Dislocated shoulders were treated by bonesetters, and ...oken legs were put in harnesses.

AFTER THEM!
Upper-class women were also avid hunters. In this illustration of about 1340 a lady blows a hunting horn as she gallops after the dogs.

WEAPON AT THE READY
The crossbow was a popular hunting weapon. It could be used on horseback and easily reloaded using a goat's-foot lever or a ratchet-and-winder mechanism called a rack. The bowstring was drawn back over the nut and held there until released by the trigger, the crossbow could be kept drawn tight in case any game was flushed out.
Crossbows for use in hunting were sometimes lavishly decorated. On this example of 1450–1470 the owner's coat of arms is painted on the tiller, and there are carved panels showing hunting scenes.

Original bow string of twisted cord

BOAR-CATCHER
The boar spear was a stout weapon intended to stop an onrushing boar or even a bear. To keep the blade from going too far into the animal, a crossbar was provided. Boar-sword blades were also pierced for a crossbar.

The tusks of the aggressive boar were highly dangerous

Faith and pilgrimage

THE CHURCH PLAYED A MAJOR PART in the life of the Middle Ages.
Western Europe was Roman Catholic until Protestantism took
hold in some countries in the 16th century. Most
people held strong beliefs and churches flourished,
taking one-tenth of everyone's goods as a sort of
tax called a tithe. Monasteries were sometimes
founded by wealthy lords, partly to make up for
their sins. Some lords actually became monks
after a life of violence, hoping that this would make
it easier for them to enter heaven. To get help from
dead saints, Christians would make pilgrimages to well-
known shrines, such as the tomb of St. Peter in Rome, and wear
a symbolic badge. Holy relics, many of them forgeries, were carried
for protection.

OWNER OF THE HORN
This medallion shows
Charles, Duke of
Burgundy, who owned
the Horn of St. Hubert
in the late 15th century.

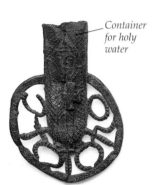

*Container
for holy
water*

WATER CARRIER
People wore ampullae, tiny
containers holding holy water,
to protect themselves from evil.
This one has a picture of St.
Thomas Becket, killed at
Canterbury in 1170, and would
have been bought after a
pilgrimage to his shrine.

*Lead pilgrim badge
of St. Catherine
martyred on a
wheel*

KNIGHT AT PRAYER
The saints played a vital part in peoples' lives.
This stained-glass window from the Netherlands
shows a knight from the Bernericourt family
praying at a statue of Mary Magdalene.

*Lead seal showing
the Virgin Mary
holding baby
Jesus*

SYMBOLS OF FAITH
People often wore
badges to show that they
had been on a pilgrimage.
The simple lead cross shows
the importance of this sign –
even a knight's sword guard
could be used as a cross. Other
popular subjects were Christ, the
Virgin Mary, and the saints.

SILVER CHAL
A chalice was used
hold the consecra
wine during the ma
This one, which v
made in Spain or Italy
the early 16th century. Its r
decoration shows the wealth a
importance of the church. I
decorated with six medallio
which show Christ and so
of the saints, including
James of Composte
Pilgrims to his to
wore badges beari
his emblem
scallop sh

Head of saint

HORN OF ST. HUBERT

Medieval people liked to touch or even possess relics of the dead saints, even though some had no connection with the real saint. St. Hubert was said to have seen the vision of a cross shining between a deer's antlers, and he became the patron saint of huntsmen.

Pelican in her piety

St. John

Virgin Mary

Crucified Christ

TO BE A PILGRIM

These 15th-century pilgrims are traveling to the Holy Land. Jerusalem, where Christ was crucified and buried, was the greatest goal, but getting there meant a long and dangerous journey. Pilgrims who returned from Jerusalem were called palmers and wore a palm-leaf badge.

MISSIONARY

The Church was always eager to convert others to Christianity, either through peaceful teaching or by more forceful methods like those used by the Teutonic Knights in Eastern Europe. Here a friar called Oderic receives a blessing before he goes to the East as a missionary. Knights might also desire a blessing before undertaking dangerous tasks or journeys.

THE CANTERBURY TALES

Geoffrey Chaucer (right) wrote *The Canterbury Tales* in the late 1300s. These concern a group of pilgrims who travel from London to the shrine of Thomas Becket in Canterbury. A knight (left) and his son, a squire, join the group, who tell stories along the way to pass the time.

Chaucer's knight

Geoffrey Chaucer

St. Nicholas

PROCESSIONAL CROSS

This early-15th-century Italian silver cross has been partly gilded and decorated with enamel. The Virgin Mary, St. John, and St. Nicholas are shown on the arms of the cross. The pelican is a symbol of piety: People thought that she wounded herself in order to feed her young, like Christ bleeding for all sinners.

The Crusades

In 1095 AT CLERMONT, FRANCE, Pope Urban II launched a military expedition to take the Christian holy places in Jerusalem back from the Seljuk Turks who ruled the Holy Land. This expedition became known as the First Crusade. A huge army traveled thousands of miles across Europe, gathering at Constantinople (now Istanbul) before going on to capture Jerusalem in 1099. But the city was soon retaken by the Muslims, and many other crusades failed to take it back, apart from a brief period in 1229 when the German emperor Frederick II made an agreement with the Muslims. Even Richard Lionheart, the warlike English king and a leader of the Third Crusade of 1189–1192, knew that if he could capture the city, he would not be able to hold it. Nevertheless, Western leaders set up feudal states in the Holy Land. The fall of Acre in 1291 marked the end of one of these states. But Christians still fought Muslims in Spain and the Mediterranean. Crusades were also preached against non-Catholic heretics in Europe.

PEOPLE'S CRUSADE
In 1096 the French preacher Peter the Hermit led an undisciplined mob from Cologne in Germany toward Jerusalem. On their way they pillaged and looted, killing Jews for their money and because they thought them responsible for Christ's death. Though there were some knights in this People's Crusade, it was wiped out in Anatolia (modern Turkey) by the Turks.

SPANISH CRUSADERS
Muslims, known as Moors, had lived in Spain since the eighth century. From the 11th century on, Christian armies tried to push them back south; Granada, their last stronghold, fell to the Christians in 1492. Warrior monks, such as the Order of Santiago, seen in this 13th-century picture, helped the Christian reconquest of Spain.

Border of crowns

KING ON A TITLE
Medieval churches were often decorated with patterned ceramic tiles. These examples come from Chertsey Abbey, England. They bear a portrait of Richard I, known as Richard Lionheart, who was king of England from 1189 to 1199, and was one of the leaders of the Third Crusade of 1190.

TAKING SHIP
To get from Europe to the Holy Land, people could either take the dangerous road overland, or cross the Mediterranean Sea. The Italian city-states of Venice, Pisa, and Genoa, eager for new trade, often provided ships. Unfortunately, in 1203 Venice persuaded the leaders of the Fourth Crusade to attack the Byzantine capital of Constantinople, which never recovered.

THE MAMLUKS
An elite body of troops, the Mamluks were slaves recruited by the Muslims. This late 13th- or early 14th-century bronze bowl shows a mounted Mamluk heavy cavalryman. He appears to be wearing a lamellar cuirass, a type of armor that was made from small iron plates laced together. Above his head he holds a slightly curved saber.

Mamluk cavalryman

Arabic inscription

A SARACEN
Many Saracens (nomadic Muslims) used fast horses and shot arrows at the Crusaders from their recurved composite bows. Some wore forms of plate armor but many wore mail or padded defenses. Round shields were common, and curved slashing sabers became popular in the 12th century.

TURKISH WARRIOR
This Italian dish of about 1520 shows a Turkish warrior. The crusades died out in the early 14th century and the great fortified city of Constantinople (now Istanbul) stood between Turkey and the mainland of Europe. However, the city never fully recovered from the damage it suffered during the Fourth Crusade in 1204. In 1453 it finally fell to the Sultan Suleyman the Magnificent. It has remained part of Turkey ever since.

FIGHTING FOR THE FAITH
This mid-13th-century picture shows Christians and Muslims clashing in 1218 during the Christian siege of Damietta at the mouth of the Nile in Egypt. The artist has dressed the Muslims (on the right) much like Christians.

STRONGHOLDS IN THE EAST
The Crusaders built stone castles and borrowed some ideas from examples in the East. Crusader castles were built on strong natural sites when possible. This huge castle, Krak des Chevaliers in Syria, was held by the Knights Hospitalers. An outer ring of walls was added in the 13th century.

CROSS-LEGGED KNIGHT
This effigy, carved in the late 13th century, was said to be that of English knight Sir John Holcombe, who died of wounds during the Second Crusade (1147-1149). The cross-legged pose is often thought to indicate a Crusader. In fact it is simply a style used by the sculptors of the time.

Knights of Christ

I N 1118 A BAND OF KNIGHTS who protected Christian pilgrims in the Holy Land were given quarters near the Temple of Jerusalem. These men, the Knights Templars ("of the temple"), became a religious order but differed from other monks by remaining warriors and continuing to fight the Muslims. In the same period another order of monks, who had worked with the sick, became a military order called the Knights of St. John or Knights Hospitalers. When the Christians lost control of the Holy Land in 1291 the Templars, by now less active, found that the European rulers who had supported them did not like their wealth, power, and their lack of action, and they were disbanded. The Hospitalers moved their base to the Mediterranean and continued fighting the Muslims. The Teutonic Knights, a German order that had become military in 1198, moved to Eastern Europe and forced the Slavs to convert to Christianity.

Position of original spout

MEDICINE JA
The Hospitaler used jars mad from decorate pottery called majolic to hold their medicine Although a military orde these monks had been carin for the sick since the 11t century and continued to d so while also providir fighting men for th Christian wars agains the Muslim

THE HOSPITAL
Malta was the final home of the Knights of St. John. This engraving of 1586 shows them at work on the great ward of their hospital in the Maltese capital, Valletta.

BRONZE MORTAR
Ingredients for Hospitaler medicines were ground by a pestle in this mortar dating from the 12th or 13th century.

BURNING THE TEMPLARS

After the Christians took control of the Holy Land, the Templars became very rich and powerful, which made them unpopular. King Philip IV of France decided to seize their wealth. The grand master, Jacques de Molay, was killed in 1314 and the order was suppressed in Europe.

THE FIGHT GOES ON

After the loss of the Holy Land in 1291, the Hospitalers moved first to Cyprus, then in 1310 to Rhodes where they again clashed with the Muslims. This continual struggle meant that despite their wealth, they managed to escape the fate of the Templars.

GRAND MASTER'S SEAL

A grand master led each military order. This seal belonged to Raymond de Berenger, who ruled the Hospitalers from 1363–1374.

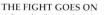

PROCESSIONAL CROSS

This early 16th-century cross is made of oak covered with silver plate. The figure of Christ is older. The Evangelists are pictured on the arms of the cross. The cross belonged to the Hospitalers and the coat of arms is that of Pierre Decluys, Grand Prior of France from 1522–1535. Each military order had priories or commanderies in several countries to raise money and recruits.

ORDER OF SERVICE *above*

The Knights of St. John were expected to attend church services and to know their Bible in the same way as other monks. Breviaries like this one contained the daily service. The religious knights had to obey strict rules, which were usually based on those of the regular monastic orders. Hospitalers followed the rule of St. Benedict, the Templars that of the Cistercian order.

KNIGHT TEMPLAR

Templars wore a white surcoat (tunic) with a red cross. In this 12th-century fresco from the Templar church at Cressac, France, a knight gallops into battle.

THE RHODES MISSAL

Joining the Knights Hospitaler meant being a skilled fighting man yet rejecting the world for a monastic life. Like other monks, the knights swore to serve the order faithfully, to remain chaste, and to help those in need. It is thought that many knights took their vows on this book, the late-15th-century Rhodes Missal.

WATER BOTTLE

A water supply was vital in the heat of the Mediterranean and along pilgrim routes in the Holy Land. This metal water bottle of about 1500 bears the cross of the Order of St. John.

Knights of the Rising Sun

Europe was not the only area to have a warrior class. Japan developed a society similar to the feudal system of medieval Europe, and the equivalent of the knight was the samurai. Like a Western knight he was a warrior, often fighting on horseback, serving a lord and served by others in turn. After the Gempei War of 1180-1185 Japan was ruled by an emperor, but real power lay with the shogun, or military leader. However, civil wars had weakened the Shogun's power by 1550, and Japan was split into kingdoms ruled by daimyo or barons. In 1543 Portuguese merchants brought the first guns to Japan; soon large, professional armies appeared. A strong shogun was revived after a victory in 1600, and the last great samurai battle was fought in 1615.

HELMET AND FACE GUARD
Helmets like this 17th-century example are often fi
with mustaches. They have a neckguard made of i
plates coated with lacquer (a type of varnish) an
laced together with silk. Lacquer was used to prot
metal from moisture in the humid climate of Japa

EARLY ARMOR *above*
This 19th-century copy of a 12th-century armor is in the *O-yoroi*, or "great armor," style. An iron strip is attached to the top of the breast, and the rest of the cuirass is made of small lacquered iron plates laced together with silk and leather. The 12th-century samurai who wore armor like this were basically mounted archers.

FIGHTING SAMURAI
These two samurai are fighting on foot. From the 14th century on, there was an increase in this type of combat, although samurai still fought on horseback when necessary. The shift toward foot combat with sword and curved spear brought changes in the armor.

SWORDSMAN
Samurai prized their swords greatly. This 19th-century print shows a samurai holding his long sword unsheathed. His smaller sword is thrust through his belt, with the cutting edge uppermost to deliver a blow straight from the scabbard.

Tempered edge

PAIR OF SWORD
The main samurai sword wa the *katana*, sheathed in a woode scabbard (*saya*). The guard for the hilt wa formed by a decorated oval metal plate (*tsuba*). The gr (*tsuka*) was covered in rough sharkskin, to prevent the har slipping, and bound with silk braid. A pommel cap (*kashira*) fitte over the end. The pair of swords (*daisho*) was completed by a short sword (*wakizashi*), which was also stuck through the be

MASTER AND SERVANT

A small lacquered case, or *inro*, is decorated with a picture of a servant kneeling before a samurai. Just like western knights, warriors needed servants to attend them and look after their equipment. A samurai held life-and-death power over his servants and over the farmers who worked on his land and provided him with food.

MODERN ARMOR

From the 16th century on, Japanese armor was made more solid, in a bid to give more protection from bullets. This example is a 19th-century armor called a *tosei gusoku*. A *do*, or cuirass, protects the chest, each arm has a defense (*kote*) and shoulder guard (*sode*); and each leg has armor for the lower thigh (*haidate*) and shin (*suneate*). The helmet (*kabuto*) has a face defense (*mempo*) and is fitted with a buffalo-horn crest.

HE ART OF SWORDSMANSHIP

this section from a 19th-century
cture by Kunisada, a samurai
lled Minamoto Yoshitsune is
structed in swordplay by
eatures called *Tengi*. Learning to
e the sword correctly took many
ars of hard work; the swordsman
d many moves to perfect.
panese swords had extremely
arp cutting edges.

Sharkskin grip

WARRIOR

This 19th-century photograph shows a samurai dressed in his armor. This is made of solid plates of iron, unlike the earlier small laced plates. Over his armor he wears a *jinbaori*, or surcoat. He carries not only his swords but also a long bow made of bamboo and other woods glued together and bound with rattan. His helmet crest bears a pair of horns.

The professionals

IN THE HEAT OF BATTLE even heavily armed squadrons of knights could not break the disciplined ranks of infantry. The wars between France and Burgundy in 1476–1477 showed how mounted knights were unable to defeat solid bodies of pikemen backed up by soldiers using handguns. So by 1500 the infantry was becoming the most important part of any army. In Germany foot soldiers called *Landsknechte* copied their Swiss neighbors in using pikes and guns. The way men were hired was also changing. Feudal forces, who fought in return for their land, were increasingly being replaced by paid permanent forces of well-trained soldiers backed up by mercenaries and men recruited locally. Although mounted knights still played their part, they were becoming less effective on the battlefield.

PUFFED AND SLASHED ARMOR
In the late 15th and early 16th centuries the Swiss and German Landsknechte enjoyed showing off by wearing extravagant clothing in the "puffed and slashed" style. This German armor made in about 1520 mimics that style. The slashings are etched and gilt, whereas the surfaces in between are etched to suggest damask or cut-velvet cloth.

Bellows visor

Later mail

HANDGUNNERS
Late-15th-century Swiss handgunners, backed up by wheeled cannon, fire matchlock pistols at enemy soldiers. Already Swiss armies consisted largely of infantry pike formations supported by units of handgunners and cannon.

Steel strips to guard inside of elbow

Puffed and slashed decoration

CAT-GUTTER
This German *Landsknecht* of about 1520 wears partial armor with puffed and slashed breeches, and a "bishop" mantle" of mail to guard his neck. As well as a two-handed sword he carries a distinctive short sword that was called a *Katzbalger* (cat-gutter).

Grip covered in wood and leath

Crossguard

Lug

Ricasso wit leather covering

"Flamboya – wavy – e

TWO-HANDED SWORD
Swords like thi were useful for cutting the poi off pikes carrie by enemy soldiers. The lu on the blade helped keep an enemy weapon from sliding u to the hands. T leather coverin the ricasso, or blunted sectio on the blade, allowed a shor grip on the weapon. This example is fro 1600, by which time these wer becoming ceremonial weapons.

IN BLACK AND WHITE

Infantrymen who could afford some protection often chose a half armor, omitting leg pieces so they could walk easily. Light horsemen wore similar armor. The open helmet, called a burgonet, let more air get to the face. The black-and-white effect on this armor of about 1550 was made by leaving some areas as bright steel while painting other parts black. The paint was also thought to protect against rust.

HALBERD

The heavy ax head on this infantry staff weapon could be used to maim an enemy, while the beak on the back could trip up horses or hook a knight from the saddle. This German example dates to about 1500.

Cheek piece of burgonet

Gauntlet

GERMAN CROSSBOW

This crossbow of about 1520 has a bow made from cane and whalebone covered with parchment. When the short crossbow bolt struck armor squarely it could punch through it. Unlike longbows, which needed constant practice, crossbows were spanned mechanically (pp. 50–51) and could be used more easily. They were popular on the European mainland.

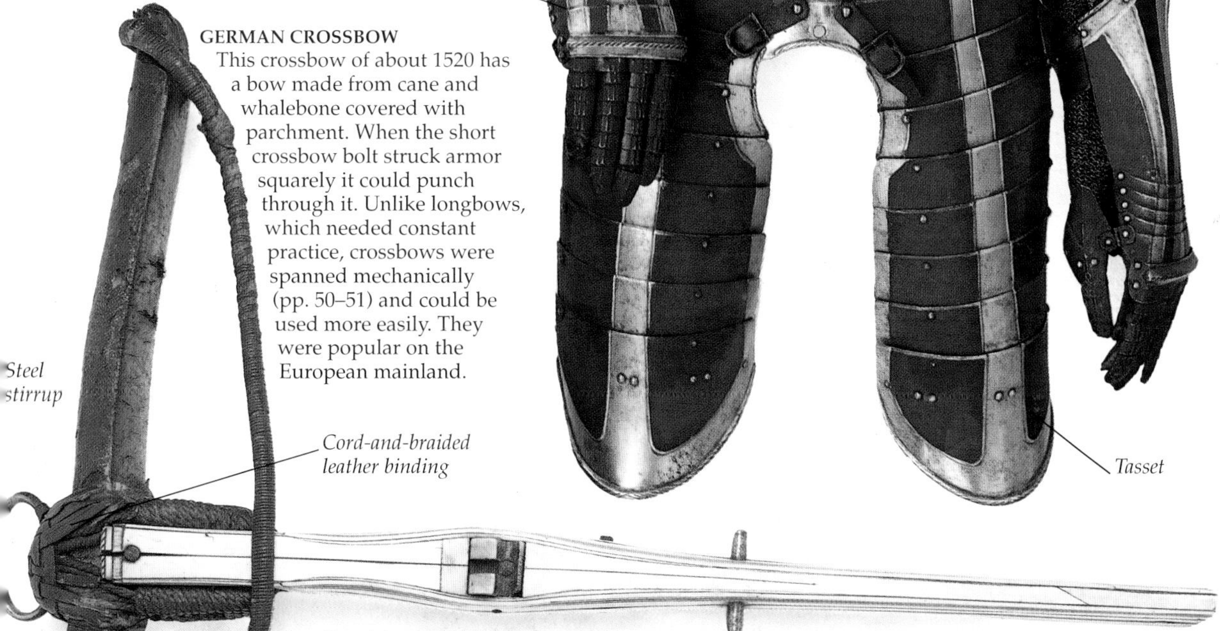

Steel stirrup

Cord-and-braided leather binding

Tasset

Bowstring of twisted cord

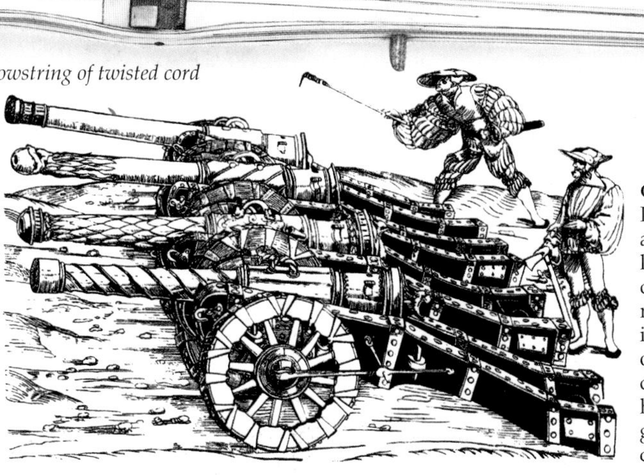

GUN BATTERY

In this woodcut of about 1520, a gunner lowers a glowing linstock to the touchhole of a cannon. The barrels have moulded decoration. The increasing use of cannon was one factor in the decline of the castle and the rise of the heavily gunned fortress. Field guns were used against enemy cavalry and infantry.

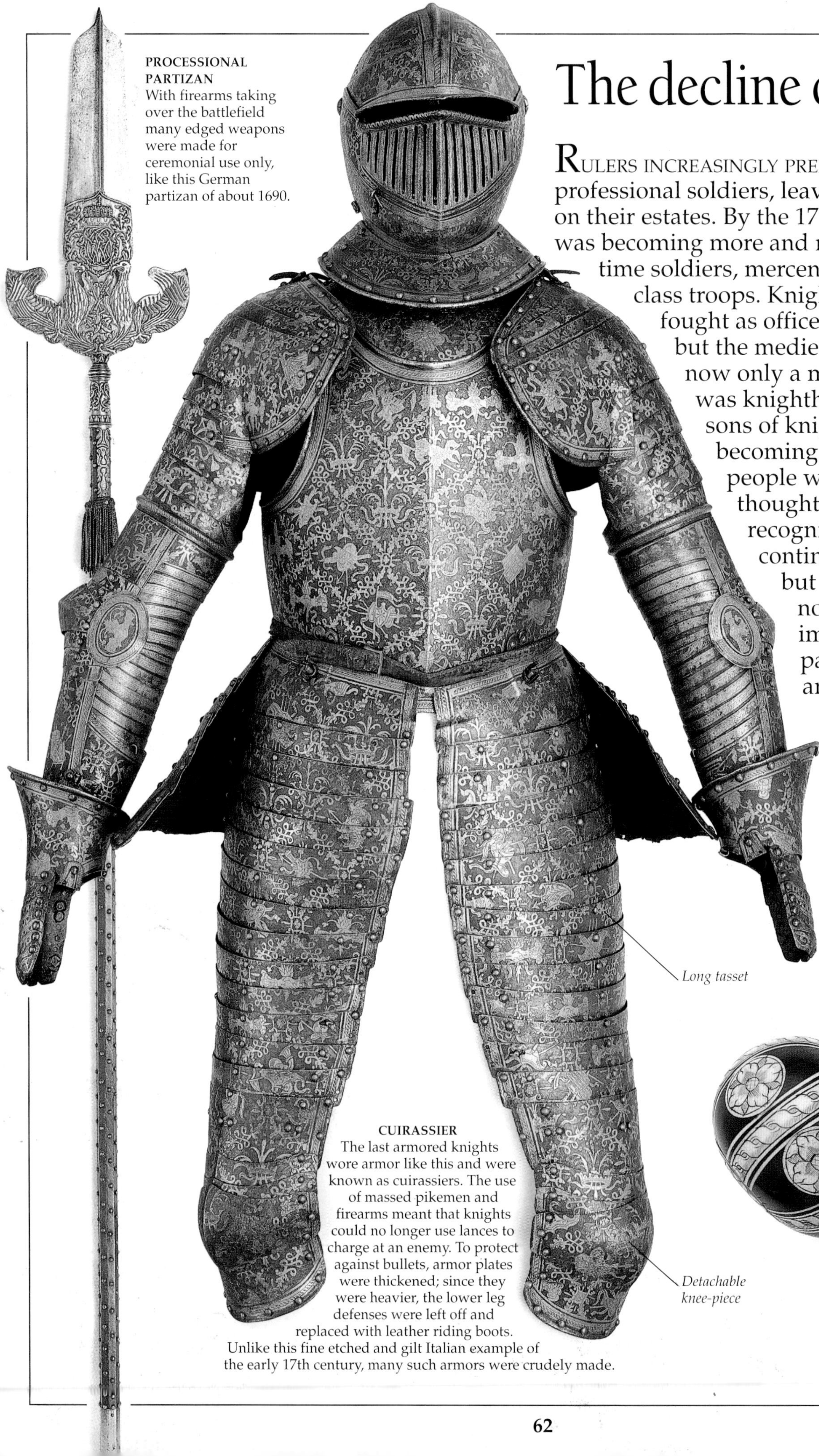

PROCESSIONAL PARTIZAN
With firearms taking over the battlefield many edged weapons were made for ceremonial use only, like this German partizan of about 1690.

Rᴜʟᴇʀꜱ ɪɴᴄʀᴇᴀꜱɪɴɢʟʏ ᴘʀᴇꜰᴇʀʀᴇᴅ to use professional soldiers, leaving knights to live on their estates. By the 17th century, warfare was becoming more and more the job of full-time soldiers, mercenaries, and middle-class troops. Knights occasionally fought as officers, usually of cavalry but the medieval fighting man wa now only a memory. No longer was knighthood only granted to sons of knights. It was becoming an honor given to people who the monarch thought deserved recognition. This idea still continues in many places, but the knight of old ha not been forgotten. Hi image survives, helpe partly by old castles and stories of heroes such as King Arthu The magic, woven by medieval poets and 19th-century romantics, lives on.

Grip

Long tasset

CUIRASSIER
The last armored knights wore armor like this and were known as cuirassiers. The use of massed pikemen and firearms meant that knights could no longer use lances to charge at an enemy. To protect against bullets, armor plates were thickened; since they were heavier, the lower leg defenses were left off and replaced with leather riding boots. Unlike this fine etched and gilt Italian example of the early 17th century, many such armors were crudely made.

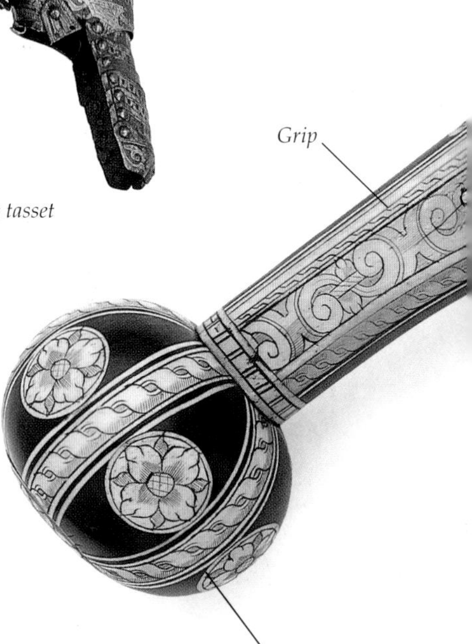

Detachable knee-piece

Butt could be used as a club

OLD VERSUS NEW *right*
This engraving of 1632 shows how an armored cuirassier with a lance could be stopped by an infantryman with a musket. Notice the wheel-lock pistol, a more effective weapon for the horseman, hanging in its holster from the saddle.

PREPARING TO FIRE *left*
An early-17th-century Dutch musketeer pours a measured amount of gunpowder from his powder flask into his musket.

Piece of rock which strikes metal to make a spark; this lights the gunpowder and fires the gun

BUFF COAT
Light cavalrymen found that a coat of soft, thick buff leather was able to stop a sword cut and was more comfortable than full armor. It was worn either alone or with a breastplate and backplate. At this time, breastplates were usually "proofed," or tested, by being shot at before they were worn.

DON QUIXOTE
Miguel de Cervantes, of Spain, wrote *Don Quixote* in the early 1600s. The novel tells of a foolish old man who jousts with windmills thinking they are giants and treats a peasant girl as his lady. He feels a sad yearning for lost knightly ideals and chivalry.

WHEEL-LOCK PISTOL
With better-quality gunpowder and larger numbers of soldiers being armed with guns, there was little place for the armored knight. Cuirassiers and light cavalry carried two wheel-lock pistols. This German example of about 1590 has an ebony stock inlaid with engraved panels and strips of stag's horn.

Ramrod

Key cylinder

ewdriver

Y
s German wrench of about 1620
und up a spring on the wheel lock
ich, when released by the sear, or
ger, spun a wheel and lowered the
k against it, causing a shower of
rks to ignite the gunpowder.

Swivel eye for suspension

Pivoting pricker to unblock vent

This late-16th-century cartridge box was designed to hang from a belt

THE VICTOR
The chivalrous ideal knight is shown about to receive his prize on this Victorian silhouette. The knight in shining armor, the quest for the Holy Grail, and other legendary Arthurian adventures appealed to the romantic Victorian mind.

Index

Acknowledgments

Dorling Kindersley would like to thank:
The Wallace Collection, the Royal Armouries, the British Museum, and the Museum of the Order of St. John for provision of objects for photography; English Heritage, the National Trust, and Cadw (Welsh Historical Monuments), for permission to photograph at Rochester, Bodiam, and Caerphilly Castles; David Edge for information; Paul Cannings, Jonathan Waller, John Waller, Bob Dow, Ray Monery, and Julia Harris for acting as models; Anita Burger for make-up; Joanna Cameron for illustrations (pages 22-23); Angels and Burmans for costumes; Sharon Spencer and Manisha Patel for design assistance; Helena Spiteri for editorial assistance; Céline Carez for research.

Picture credits

t=top, b=bottom, c=center, l=left, r=right

Ancient Art & Architecture Collection: 58cl, 58c. 58tr, 59bl
Bridgeman Art Library: 53b;54c; /Biblioteca Estense, Modena: 10b; /British Library: 19tc, 20tr, 20c, 38cr, 39c, 49tr, 54tl;/Bibliotheque Municipal de Lyon: 55c;/Bibliotheque Nationale, Paris: 11br, 15tr, 22cr, 25tl, 41tr, 42bl, 43t, 54bl, 57tr/Corpus Christi College, Cambridge: 13rc;/Corpus Christi College, Oxford: 54br;/Giraudon/ Musee Conde, Chantilly: 50bl;/51bl; / Vatican Library, Rome: 50br;/Victoria & Albert Museum 37cl;/Wrangham Collection: 59c
Burgerbibliothek, Bern: 25rc
Christ Church, Oxford/Photo: Bodleian

Library:27tl
E.T. Archive: 6bl, 11tl, 18bl, 27tr, 30bl, 31bl, 33cl, 33cr, 39tr, 41c, 49bl, 57bc, 58rc, 59cl, 60c;/Btitish Library:19bc, 32c; /British Museum:27bl;/Fitzwilliam Museum, Cambridge: 48rc
Robert Harding Picture Library: 8tl, 12rc, 18tr, 22bl, 26c, 34br, 34bl, 55bl;/British Library: 11c, 34cl, 44b, 45bl
Michael Holford: 8bl, 9tr, 52c, 55br
Hulton-Deutsch Collection: 56cl
A.F. Kersting: 9cl
Mansell Collection: 11bl, 21lc, 39tr, 46br, 55tl, 63bl,/Alinari: 46tr
Bildarchiv Foto Marburg: 48br
Arxiu Mas: 54cl
Stadtbibliothek Nurnberg: 17rc
Osterreichische Nationalbibliothek, Vienna, (Cod.2597, f.15): 40br
Pierpont Morgan Library, New York: 29c
Scala: 7br, 33t, 34tlc. 36cl
Stiftsbibliothek St Gallen: 6c

Syndication International: 26br, 27cl, 27tcl, 32bc, 37tl, 41tl, 50tr, 53l, 57tl; /Photo. Trevor Wood: 36tr
Courtesy of the Board of Trustees of the Victoria & Albert Museum: 54b.

Every effort has been made to trace the copyright holders and we apologize in advance for any unintentional omissions. We would be pleased to inse the appropriate acknowledgment in an subsequent edition of this publication.

j940.1
DAN

Grauett, Christopher
Dann, Geoff.

Knight.

DATE DUE

MAR 1 4 2019

NOV 1 5 2018

AUG 2 0 2015

OCT 1 1 2001